Qigong for health & vitality

Qigong for health & vitality

Michael Tse

PIATKUS

Acknowledgements

Writing a book is not easy, writing a good book is particularly difficult. I hope this book will raise some interest and be of benefit to you, the reader. In writing it, I have tried to open a door to the Qigong world and to make the first few steps into that world easier. I hope you will forgive me if I have made any mistakes as I am aware that there is always more to learn and I certainly do not claim to know everything.

Finally, I would like to thank my team, friends, students and publisher, including: Darryl Tam, Irmgard Niermann, Penny Ramsden, John Hayes, Daniel Poon, Ray Bagnal, Jessica Cowen, Anne Lawrance, Gill Cormode, and Fai at Final Film, who have all helped me to complete this book.

The photographs on page 15 are courtesy of Tim Malyon and Paul Biddle/Science Photo Library (top) and The Hutchinson Library.

For the latest news and information on all our titles, visit our website at www.piatkus.co.uk

First published in 1995 by
Judy Piatkus (Publishers) Ltd
5 Windmill Street, London W1T 2JA
email: info@piatkus.co.uk

Reprinted 1995, 1997, 1998
Reisssued 2001

The moral right of the author has been asserted

A catalogue record for this book
is available from the British Library

ISBN 0–7499–1336–3

Edited by Esther Jagger
Designed by Paul Saunders
Photography by Jon Stewart
Illustrations by One-Eleven Line Art

Set in Sabon by Selwood Systems, Midsomer Norton
Printed and bound in Great Britain by
Butler & Tanner Ltd, Frome and London

Contents

About the Author

Michael Tse was born in Hong Kong in February 1960. He has spent twenty of his thirty-five years studying and training with some of the most famous and respected teachers and healers in China.

His first introduction to healing was while studying with his uncle who worked in traditional Chinese medicine as a bonesetter and herbalist. His uncle was teaching him the martial art of Wing Chun and as part of his training Michael was made to perform the first form very slowly. It was during this practice that Michael first became aware of the energy (Qi) moving in his body. This feeling was enough to stimulate his interest in the internal arts and Qigong in particular. This interest soon became a passion which took up more and more of his time until eventually the study of the many facets of Qigong led Michael to make it his life's work.

His timing couldn't have been better. Much of the real cultural heritage that China had to offer was being rediscovered by the Chinese people themselves after what had been an extremely turbulent period in their history. Many teachers who had previously only shared their skills and abilities with small, closed communities were now taking selected students so that these skills could be perpetuated and the benefits passed to a wider audience. One such teacher was a lady by the name of Yang Mei Jun (see page 5) who is the inheritor of the Daoist Dayan Qigong. Michael's search for the very best teachers led him to this remarkable woman and he was accepted by her as a close student, something of an accolade in Chinese society.

A resident of England since 1988, Michael now combines running private clinics for the treatment of a broad range of illnesses with teaching Chinese health exercises (Qigong) and martial arts (Chen Taiji Quan and Wing Chun). He conducts seminars and demonstrates his skills throughout the world while also offering consultancy and training to a variety of organisations. He maintains an intensive personal training schedule in order to retain his high standards and to guarantee the quality and effectiveness of his teachings.

At his clinics in Harley Street, London and St John Street, Manchester, Michael puts into practice many of the skills that he has learnt, giving advice and encouraging people to take charge of their illnesses. The patients who come to Michael's clinic suffer from a variety of illnesses including hypertension, M.E., cancer, arthritis, angina, diabetes, back problems, obesity, stomach ulcers, asthma, eczema, liver conditions, strokes, bronchitis and chronic pain. Michael's personal philosophy, which he often quotes, is '*You* are your own best healer' and he stimulates his patients' internal energy so that their *own* bodies can maximise their innate and powerful healing potential. The empowerment of the patient is crucial in Qigong healing as the healer and patient work together.

Michael has now dedicated his life to conveying the benefits of daily Qigong practice and in doing so has established the Tse Qigong Centre (see page 134) which offers training to a high level of mastership in many skills. Anyone who has attended one of his seminars will appreciate that he is a great believer in using knowledge to deepen one's experience, lending more form and insight into the movement and meditation skills that he teaches. Apart from his many physical skills, he has also developed his knowledge of Feng Shui and the Yi Jing (*I-Ching*) making them an integral part of his life.

About three years ago Michael and his team launched *Qi Magazine* which regularly publishes articles related to many aspects of Chinese culture and has proved successful in establishing a network of readers interested in those skills. The magazine now has subscribers all over the UK, America, Australia, Brazil, France, Spain, Hong Kong, Germany and Croatia, and the circulation grows with each issue.

Probably his greatest skill as a communicator is to take complex concepts and present them in a readily accessible and interesting way. I think you will appreciate this once you have read his book.

John Hayes
The Tse Qigong Centre

Introduction

In China, in the early morning from five to nine o'clock, you can see hundreds of people exercising in the parks or at the side of the roads. You might think they were practising Taiji Quan or some relaxation exercise, but it could well be Qigong (pronounced 'chee-gong'), one of the most ancient health exercises which has been passed down from generation to generation for over three thousand years.

Today, in Shanghai and Beijing, scientists are using modern equipment to research and analyse Qigong. They have found it particularly beneficial in treating chronic complaints such as hypertension, pyknocardia, asthma, arthritis, myalgic encephalomyelitis (M.E.), neurasthenia and headaches, as well as acute health conditions such as appendicitis.

But Qigong is far more than a means of improving or restoring health, valuable though that aspect undoubtedly is. Qigong also has a place in science, sport and study. People practise it during their breaks at work and after the day's work is over, in order to relax. Many athletes use Qigong before major events in order to optimise their performances: it is known, for instance, that records achieved during training often cannot be repeated because stress makes the body unstable; but Qigong can keep the mind calm and so maintain the body's stability.

Qigong is something wonderful which, although still unfamiliar to many Western people, has in recent years become magic, spreading out like heat from China all over the world. It now has devotees in America, Canada, Japan, Australia, Singapore, Malaysia, Russia and

An everyday sight in China is that of people practising Qigong in the parks.

Europe, and its popularity grows more and more every day. Part of its appeal lies in the fact that it is something that everyone, whatever their age or state of fitness, can learn and enjoy.

My aim in writing this book is to introduce you to the practice and philosophy of Qigong in a positive way and enable you to reap the benefits of improved health and vitality that it brings. I have endeavoured to make it easy to learn and easy to do, particularly for beginners. Obviously it would be impossible in such a book to deal with all the complexities of a system that has been developing for thousands of years; but if I can help you to understand what it has to offer, and to enter the world of Qigong without difficulty, then I will have gone some way towards my goal of enabling Qigong to bring a healthier life to everyone.

About the book

Qigong for Health and Vitality is divided into two parts. Part One gives an introduction to the background and philosophy of Qigong while Part Two forms the practical section. It is best to read through the whole book before starting on the exercises.

The practical section is illustrated with step-by-step photographs and consists of two forms of Qigong exercise. The first form is *Balancing Gong* which is based on animal movements and is especially good for those of us who lead increasingly sedentary lives, working in offices. The exercises will improve circulation and increase vitality. The second form I have included is *Taiji Qigong*, a series of eighteen movements derived from Taiji Quan, which can be used for self-healing. Meditation is an important part of Qigong and information and advice is given in Chapter 10.

If you wish to go to a class, ask around and seek recommendations before joining, or you can contact the Tse Qigong Centre (see page 134) which holds classes in different parts of the UK and abroad.

Finally, the occasional use of the word 'he' in the book should be taken to mean 'he or she'. It is merely to avoid clumsiness that I have refrained from spelling this out every time.

Michael Tse
September 1994

Michael Tse with his teacher Yang Mei Jun who is over 100 years old.

PART ONE

Background and Ideas

1

The Origins of Qigong

In ancient times most of the population of China consisted of peasants. The people would work in the fields all day until sunset, and then return to their homes to rest. Some would gather together and listen to the stories of their elders, while others would go and enjoy the cool night air after the heat of the day. Since the people enjoyed the refreshing nights more than the stifling days, they preferred the moon to the sun; that is why the Chinese calendar follows the moon – it is a lunar calendar, as opposed to the West's solar calendar.

Healing and wellbeing

Out in the moonlight, the weary peasants could wind down and relax. And it was then that they became aware of something moving around inside their bodies – something that felt a little like steam. This steam could move up or down, and in different places such as the legs or arms; it also seemed to be related to their breathing and to the mind. The people noted all these various feelings and eventually discovered that each person had a centre, just below the navel, which made the rest of the body warm and strong. They called this centre 'Dantien'.

With continued observation they found that the flow of the steam could make the body warm and was related to the spirit – spirit in the sense of a feeling of wellbeing rather than in the religious sense of the word. Gradually they discovered a network of channels crossing the body, linking the internal organs. Distributed along these channels were certain points which affected the way the steam flowed through the body. Thus energy (Qi) and the system of acupuncture points and channels were discovered, and people found that touching and massaging the points could heal a variety of problems.

Movement and breathing of various kinds to create heat were thus perceived as ways of healing physical ailments from very early times, long before the formulation of medicines. Throughout the centuries Chinese sages and philosophers have written of the beneficial effects of this treatment.

The Yellow Emperor's Canon of Internal Medicine, an ancient text of 722–721 BC which is known in Chinese as the *Huangdi Neijing*, contains the following passage:

> People live in the centre [of China, along the Yellow River]. The area is damp, therefore suffering from tiredness, depression and hot and cold illness [similar to today's ME – myalgic encephalomyelitis or post-viral syndrome] is common. The curing method is Daoyin [breathing techniques] and Angiao [stretching].

Even earlier than this, about four thousand years ago, the people of this region are known to have danced to rid themselves of damp and arthritis. Dancing made them hot, and the heat expelled the damp and poison from their veins and joints.

The movements and breathing patterns of animals were also regarded as valuable examples to follow. In his book *Chunway Chu*, written around 600 BC and dealing with the subject of breathing, Zhuang Zi said: 'Breathing techniques can improve metabolism; moving like a bear and a bird will result in longevity.'

During the Three Kingdoms Period (from 280–220 BC), a famous Chinese doctor, Hwa Tou, created 'Five Animal Play'. He understood how wild animals lived and how they moved to maintain their bodies' balance and he saw how people, living under the system of society, had lost this natural ability. 'Five Animal Play' was designed to help people relearn this skill in order to cure illness and strengthen the body. Hwa Tou explained that when you raised your arms above your head, as if they were the horns of a deer, it stimulated the Qi circulation of the liver; when you stretched your arms out like a bird spreading its wings, it was good for the heart and relieving tension; rubbing and slapping yourself and moving like a monkey was good

for the spleen; stretching your arms out in front of you while exhaling, like a tiger, was good for releasing the tension in the lungs; and bending forwards like the bear was good for the back and the kidneys. Hwa Tou used the names of animals because it made the exercises easier to remember and by using wild animals, instead of domestic ones, he made the exercises sound exhilarating.

All these movements help the Qi flow along the channels, strengthening the body and promoting vitality. They also balance the circulation and stimulate the internal organs.

The famous seventh-century BC philosopher Lao Zi advised people to relax their hearts (meaning their chests) and to firm their stomachs, by which he meant that they should concentrate their minds on the centre (Dantien, as mentioned above).

And so these techniques continued to be used, with great effect, for hundreds of years. In the twentieth century, while Western medicine was relying heavily on new drugs, improved surgical techniques and so on, this ancient and proven method of healing was still highly valued in the East. During the revolution of 1911, when China ceased to be ruled by emperors, Jiang Weigiao's Yin Shi Zi Sitting Still Exercises became very popular in Shanghai. Nor, to begin with, did the advent of Communism in 1949 affect the high regard in which Qigong was held. The first Qigong therapy clinic was established at Tangshan in Heibei Province in 1955, and another was set up two years later in Shanghai. That Qigong was taken seriously even in official quarters is evidenced by the fact that in 1959 the Ministry for Public Health held the First National Meeting for the Exchange of Qigong Experiences at Beidihe in Heibei Province; it was attended by some sixty-four groups from seventeen provinces, municipalities and autonomous regions from within a country as large as the USA.

Victim of the Cultural Revolution

The development and appreciation of Qigong continued unabated until 1966, when the Cultural Revolution began and most of China's traditional culture was outlawed. All study of Taoism, Confucianism and Buddhism, for instance, was prohibited; some monks and nuns were forced to abandon the religious life and were only allowed to study Marxism. Anything relating to the old way of life in China, including Qigong, was condemned or 'sent to hell', as the Chinese would say.

But Qigong survived these terrible years: it is a diamond – even after it has been attacked it lets the light shine through it into the darkness. In 1978, when the Cultural Revolution came to an end, I was living in Hong Kong. I remember seeing the 'heat' spreading throughout China. Qigong was still being practised and within three years at least five magazines devoted to Qigong were being published there.

Once the 'Gang of Four' was overthrown the ancient culture began to grow back, like grass sprouting up through the bare earth after spring rain. At first most people did their Qigong just for exercise, although some combined it with their Taiji Quan and other martial arts practice. Then doctors of traditional Chinese medicine started to join in, because their work is based on traditional medical principles like the flow of Qi, the Five Elements, and Yin and Yang (see Chapter 2). Their patients were introduced to Qigong to help them recover from their illnesses, and many improved more quickly than if they had been treated with Western medicine or even Chinese herbs. Old masters of the craft such as Yang Mei Jun, Gou Lin, Ma Li Tang and Que Ya Shui shared their families' skill to help unhealthy people, especially those who had suffered under the Cultural Revolution. At the same time, Taoist and Buddhist monks and nuns came forward to help and to perpetuate their knowledge.

Beyond healing: mind over matter

At the end of 1980, the famous Qigong Master Yan Xin held many lectures and healing sessions in which he successfully treated thousands of people. He conducted scientific research into Qigong and created a lot of enthusiasm for it. There was also a man called Chiang Bo Xing, commonly known as 'Chinese Number One Superman' who had extraordinary power. He could apparently look through people's bodies and see their skeletons, burn paper and clothes, move objects and even remove the contents from a sealed bottle. Everyone was quite nonplussed by this and it led to more people and scientists concentrating on the research and practice of Qigong to discover how it could develop human potential and abilities.

A wealth of information has been discovered. It has been found that many masters, like Yan Xin, can also transmit their Qi to heal people. Lin Hou Sheng in 1980 even transmitted his Qi to a patient who was undergoing an operation without anaesthetic. Master Yang Mei Jun, over one hundred years old, can see the colours of Qi – yellow, red, brown, green, white and so on – and can transmit energy with a fragrance of flowers. Qigong practice has also been found to develop the potential of children – it is claimed that some can read what is written on a piece of paper by just putting the paper to their ear.

Now the Chinese Government is focusing on this human potential or supernatural power to help develop 'Human Science'. In particular Chen Ken Xin, the Chinese National Research Chairman, has great faith in Qigong and is researching its relationship with human development. Government research has found that these extraordinary skills are connected with intensive Qigong practice, and are sometimes inherited. Chinese legend contains many tales about Buddha and the 'Immortals', the ancient Chinese Gods, who use magic to move things and to disappear – maybe there is some truth in these stories after all, and perhaps Qigong is the link between ancient legend and present reality.

Ho Hsien-ku, one of the Immortals.

2

Chinese Philosophy and Medicine

A balanced universe

If someone asked me, 'Do you believe in UFOs and life on other planets? Is there anyone out there?' I would say, 'Yes! I believe.' Why am I talking about UFOs and life on other planets? What have they got to do with Qigong? I will explain the connection, step by step.

When you learn about Qigong you will come to understand the basics of Chinese medicine, which uses natural methods to treat and heal and to balance the internal organs through herbs, massage, moxibustion, acupuncture (see page 23) and Qigong. The first four types of healing skill mainly depend on others giving you treatment, but Qigong is a way of self-healing. All five, however, are based on the principles of Yin and Yang – a question of balance.

In the West, people take medicines or drugs, vitamins and high-nutrition foods in an attempt to make themselves healthy. Gradually the body becomes saturated with these substances – which are already present in a healthy body – and after a while the body becomes reliant on them. As a result, if people forget to take their pills or 'health food' or other props, they become weak and tired. The body starts to lose its normal functions and can no longer produce its own energy. The search for different or stronger medicines and specialist doctors continues until there is nothing and no one left who can offer any help. What a very depressing way to try to become healthy and to treat our ailments!

Once when my mother came over to England, I took her to a fish and chip shop to try some English food. While eating she asked, 'Why

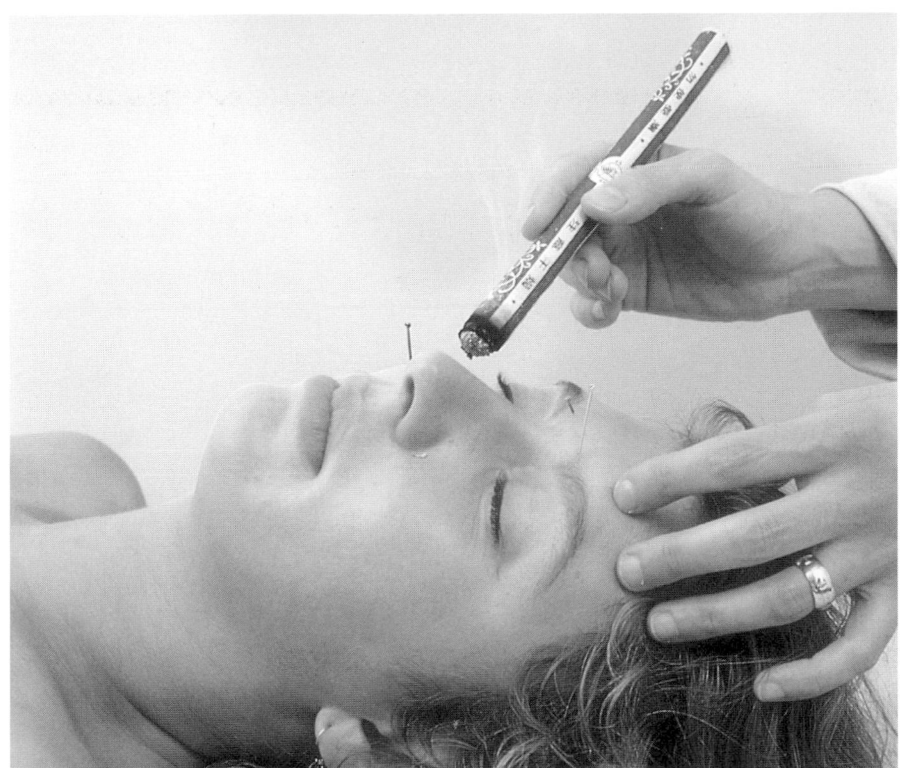

An acupuncturist using moxibustion to treat a patient. The needles are warmed with a smouldering cigar of moxa, the dried, downy covering of the leaves of Artemisia moxa.

Herbs being prepared in the traditional way.

doesn't the fish have any bones?' A good question! Fish in their natural state obviously have bones, so why don't the fish served up in fish and chip shops have any? The reason is that Western people remove the bones to make it easy to eat. Everything in modern society is geared towards making life easy so we do not need to work hard to get what we want. Eventually we will lose the natural original way to live by becoming so distanced from nature, even in the way we eat fish. Did you know that fishbones have all the essence of the nutrients? Chinese people like to suck the marrow from the bones.

The Chinese philosophy known as 'Dao' is the right way. It holds that everything has its own way, from a stone to a piece of paper to a human being. In other words, everything must be natural, and natural means balanced.

The *Scripture of Change (Yi Jing* or *I-Ching)*, which is around five thousand years old, first laid down the concept of Yin and Yang. Since then it has played a very important part in Chinese culture. The *Yi Jing* says: 'Wuji creates Taiji; Taiji creates Liang Yi, two forms; two forms create Si Xiang, four images; and four images create

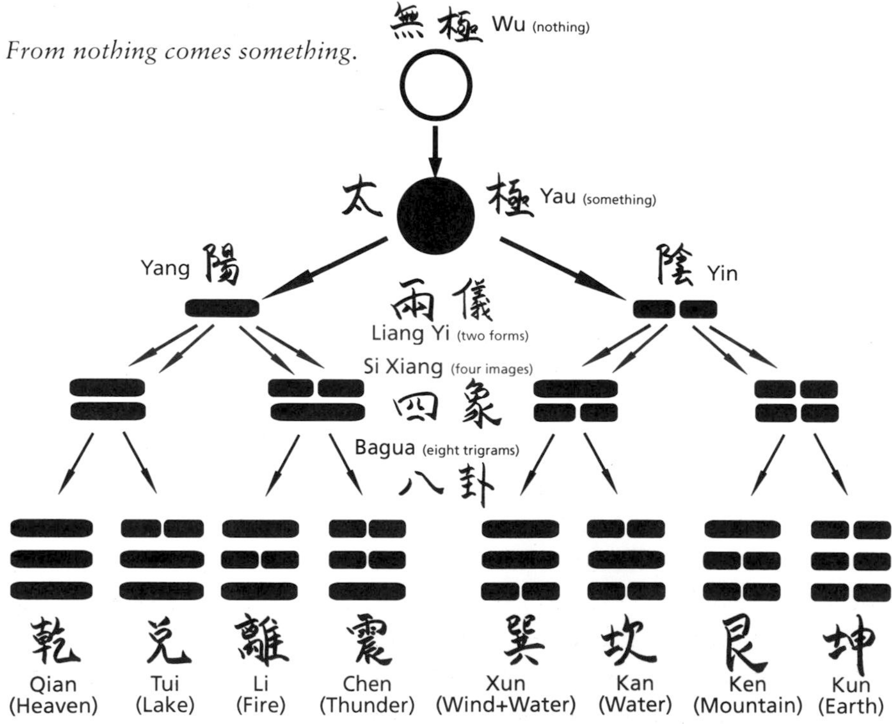

From nothing comes something.

Bagua, eight situations.' What this means is that from nothing comes something, something creates Yin and Yang, Yin and Yang create four images, and four images create eight situations.

The universe started from nothing. From nothing it became something. When something is created there must be two forms, two faces or two different situations – for instance, if one is the front there must be an opposite, the back. If one side is right, there must be a left to balance. So if we know fire, there must also be water to balance it. Male and female balance, tall and short, dark and light and so on – there are two different situations to balance the whole universe. If there is only one of something it will become too strong or too weak and will disappear by itself. For example, if there was only fire in the world, one day the world would become too hot and burn out.

'Small has no inside, big has no outside'

Nowadays many scientists spend a lot of their nation's money trying to extend the frontiers of knowledge. They want to know what is 'on the inside'. They have broken things down into molecules, atoms and electrons, smaller and smaller particles, and even sub-atomic particles. Each time they think they have found the smallest 'thing', they find another even smaller. And each time they look they find something different. It is as though these things create themselves. Modern scientists spend their working lives trying to discover new things such as the smallest or the biggest. But four thousand years ago the Chinese said in the *Yi Jing*, 'Small has no inside, big has no outside', and also: 'From nothing comes something.'

I do not know much about science, but I do know my culture – Chinese culture, which has survived for thousands of years. The principles of Yin and Yang, the Wu Xing, Five Elements, and Bagua tell us the principles of the universe. I call it 'Chinese Science' and, like Chinese medicine, it is totally different from that of the West. We use herbs which come from the earth, which is where we all come from. We use acupuncture, moxibustion and massage to stimulate different areas of the body to keep it balanced, and we practise Qigong to keep ourselves healthy, strong and vital.

We know everything must be natural. This is different from the way the West thinks. The scientists keep looking for the smallest things only to find something smaller inside, so then they look for the biggest things only to keep finding bigger things.... So they go on and on and never stop, but they miss the principle of the universe and the relationship between big and small: 'Small has no inside, big has no outside.' What is small? What is big? It is only when you put them together that one is big and one is small.

If we understand Yin and Yang we know that if we see one side then there must be another to balance it, otherwise it cannot exist (unless it is the centre). There is only one centre which is steady and stable – for example, we have only one nose and one mouth, which are at the centre of the face, but we have a pair of eyes and a pair of ears, which are not at the centre.

We live on a planet and we know that we are not at the centre of the universe. So this means there must be some other planet the same as ours in the universe, because we exist according to the principle of Yin and Yang. By developing this principle, and dividing it by two, we get the 'four images' as follows:

The Yin Yang Symbol

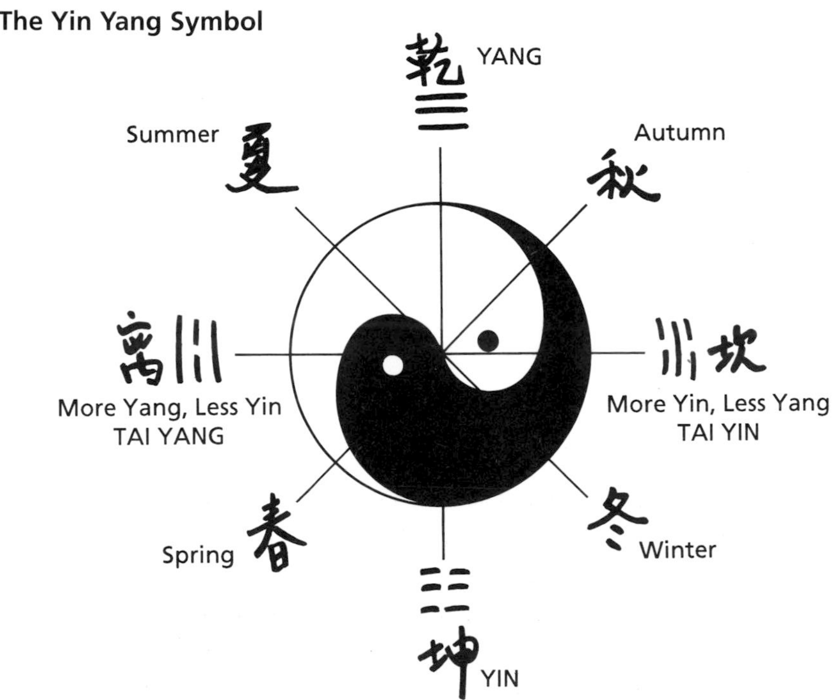

Together with the centre (which connects them all together) they become the Five Elements. So if one day you see a UFO or if we discover another human planet, don't be suprised!

The Five Elements

Wood, fire, earth, metal and water represent the Five Elements. Wood and metal form a pair: wood is Yin, soft, natural and gathering; metal is Yang, hard, polished and separating. Fire and water are another pair: water is Yin, soft, cold and flowing; fire is Yang, strong, hot and damaging. Earth is the centre, connecting all the elements, but does not belong to any of them. So earth is described as soft and wet (soil) in its Yin side, and hard and solid (rock) in its Yang side.

THE FIVE ELEMENTS AND THE DIRECTIONS

The Five Elements 'cover' the whole world. Wood represents the East, Metal the West, while Fire stands for the South and Water for the North. Earth is the centre.

The East gets the sun before the West, and so more trees and plants grow in the East. The West gets the sun later, so the West creates more minerals, metal and iron. The South is hot and the North cold.

The Five Elements and the Directions

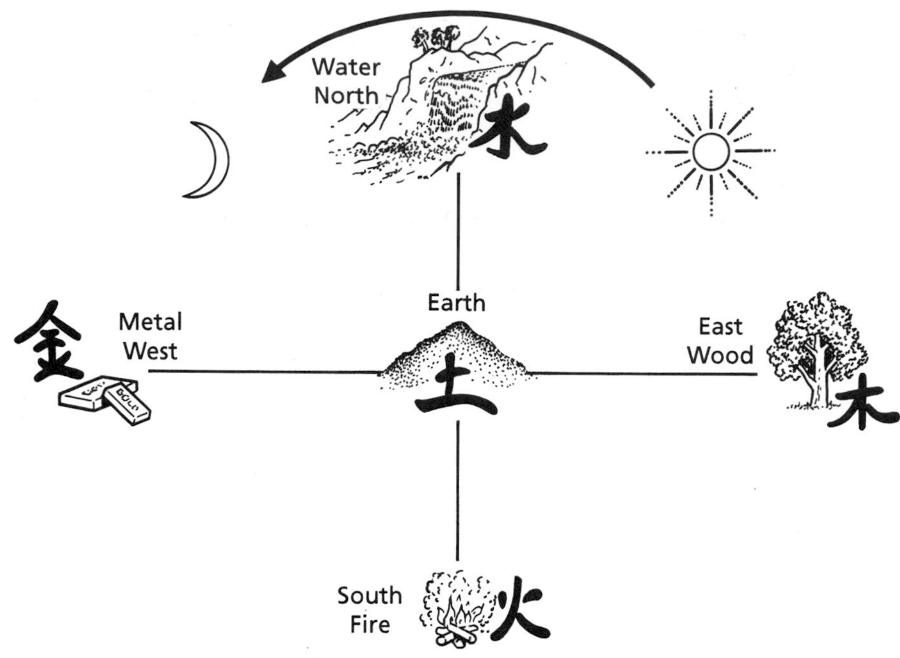

THE FIVE ELEMENTS AND THE INTERNAL ORGANS

The five elements are also associated with the five major organs that keep the entire body balanced – the liver, lungs, heart, kidneys and spleen. The main organs are all Yin and solid. They pair and work closely with the Yang organs which are hollow.

Wood is connected with the liver, and the liver with the gall bladder – they are like brothers. When you have a liver problem your face and eyes will turn green and your skin will become dry like wood. Your face will turn a greenish colour because the liver is connected with the circulation and when the liver or gall bladder is in poor condition the normal red colour of the blood will become lighter, thus turning to somewhere between green and yellow.

Metal is connected with the lungs, which are related to the large intestine. When you suffer from a lung problem it will make you cough and your face will turn white (pale) and shiny as it might if you were out of breath, after running. Also your breathing will make a noise – like metal.

Fire connects with the heart. Its brother is the small intestine. When

you have a heart problem or high blood pressure your face will go red and your body temperature will go up – hot like fire.

Water connects with the kidneys, whose brother is the urinary bladder. When you have a kidney problem or backache your face will turn a dark colour and your hands and feet will feel cold – like water. (The true colour of water is transparent, clear, but when you look at the sea it is a deep blue or closer to black.)

Earth connects to the spleen and its brother is the stomach. When you have a stomach problem, such as a stomach ache, you will feel movement inside and your stomach will make a noise. Your face will turn brown like soil and your stomach will move like an earthquake. For more on colour, see page 48.

THE FIVE ELEMENTS AND THE EMOTIONS

We are connected emotionally with the Five Elements. When you have a liver problem you will feel angry, and need to shout. By shouting you release the negative energy blocking the liver.

The Five Elements

WOOD	FIRE	EARTH	METAL	WATER
Liver	Heart	Spleen	Lung	Kidney
Gall Bladder	Small Intestine	Stomach	Large Intestine	Urinary Bladder
Green	Red/Orange	Yellow/Brown	White/Gold	Blue/Black
Shouting	Laughing	Singing/Talking	Weeping	Groaning
Anger	Joy	Over-Thinking	Sorrow, Sad	Fear
(Love, Warm)	(Stable)	(Decision)	(Happiness)	(Power and Will)
Deer	Bird	Monkey	Tiger	Bear
Sour	Bitter	Sweet	Spicy	Salty
Rancid	Scorched	Fragrant	Rotten	Putrid
Spring	Summer	Long Summer	Autumn	Winter
Tendon	Pulse	Muscle	Skin and Hair	Bone
Eye	Tongue	Mouth	Nose	Ear
Life	Gas	Compound	Solid	Liquid
East	South	Centre	West	North
Birth	Growth	Conversation	Gathering	Storage
Three	Two	Five	Four	One

When you have a heart problem your body is under pressure because your blood pressure is high. You will soon become over-excited and start laughing. Laughing releases the negative energy, easing the pressure on your heart but if you laugh *too* much, it can cause more pressure again on your heart.

When your stomach has a problem you may quickly start to worry about things and lose your appetite – or you may react in the opposite way and start to eat a lot. You like to talk to people, because talking helps you to release the negative energy and balances your stomach.

If you have a lung problem it will make you feel sad or depressed. This makes you cry easily – even just watching a sad TV programme or hearing about someone else's problem makes you cry, because crying helps you to release the tension (negative energy) from your lungs. Also, when you catch cold, the blockage in the lungs and chest will cause coughing to release the tension.

When you suffer from a kidney problem it will also affect your back. You will experience pain and feel tired. Emotionally you will feel insecure or scared. This makes you complain or moan to others or groan to yourself. But this groaning releases the negative energy from your kidneys.

From observing emotions, from how someone reacts to others and the colour of their face or even their palms, you can see which organs are causing problems. So if you find your boss likes to shout at you, forgive him (or her) as he may be suffering from a liver problem and is perhaps just releasing his negative energy. Of course, it is not good to shout at others as they will take on your negative energy. It is better to go outside on your own and shout at the trees, mountains or sea, because they can stand it. (In some Qigong practice we use sounds to strengthen the internal organs.)

Some people go to discos and dance until three or four in the morning. They think they are full of energy; actually it is not energy but over-excitement, which will affect the heart. If someone in the East is healthy and full of energy he will be calm and relaxed, he will smile and feel secure. Western people's attitude is different: if they do a lot of work, laugh a lot and are very active, they call themselves 'energetic'. In fact they are using a lot of energy, and the day might come when all that energy has been burnt out and they then become ill. Save your energy is the best advice.

Consider the Chinese interpretation of people's behaviour. You might find that a friend of yours likes to talk and eat a lot. Maybe his behaviour arises from worry caused by a stomach problem. A lot of people like to sympathise with others and cry easily in bad situations. To me, this shows that their lungs are weak. In hospital you will find many people groaning in their beds, insecure, scared of the dark and of the unknown. This is because their kidneys are weak and their energy is low.

A balanced person, however, can cope if his domestic situation or his job changes. A balanced person's mind is calm and he or she is not readily attracted by advertisements and the 'glossy things' of life. He likes nature, and knows how to relax and use his energy. The character of a healthy person is entirely different from that of an unhealthy person. A healthy person can do his job well and will be successful. Unhealthy people lose their jobs very frequently and change their situations very quickly because of their energy. Good energy can attract good people and opportunity to you. Bad energy attracts bad people and bad luck.

As you can see, the most important thing to know is how to get and stay healthy. You cannot just act healthy – you need to do something that will change your lifestyle and your character. The secret is daily Qigong practice.

Acupuncture points and channels

In the evening, when we go outside and look up, we can see crowds of sparkling stars spread all over the dark blue sky. What a wonderful picture they make. Each star has its own orbit in which it runs, keeping the whole universe balanced and the other stars in rhythm. This keeps us safe here on our planet: if a 'major' star loses its rhythm, it will affect us. Maybe the effects will only be slight or maybe they will be important: perhaps there will be a time change – twenty-six or eighteen hours in a day instead of twenty-four. Such changes would affect our balance.

Our bodies are like the universe. We too are covered by many stars. Each star has its work to do and influences the whole body and its balance. These stars are our acupuncture points, and the orbits are our acupuncture channels.

The Acupuncture Points

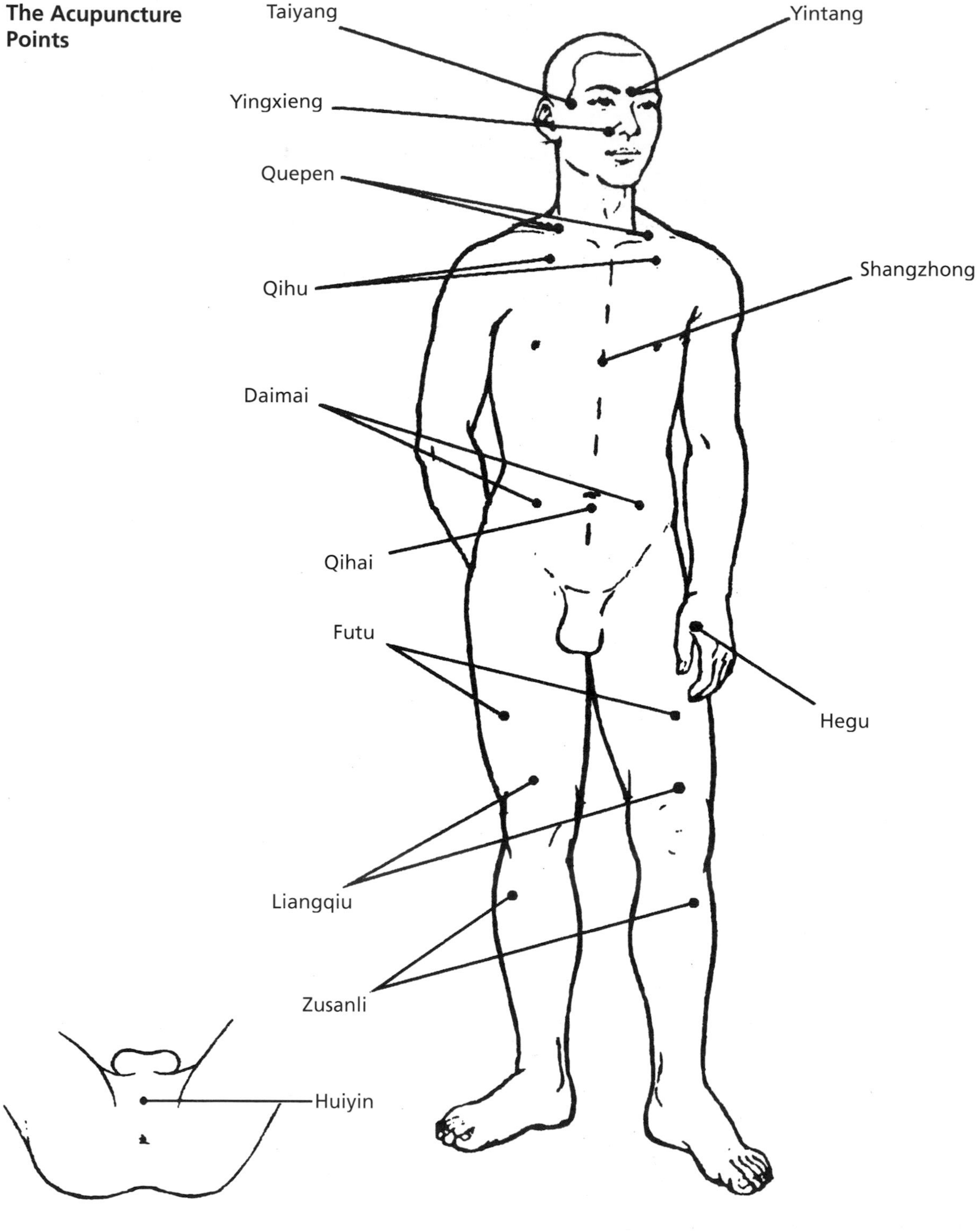

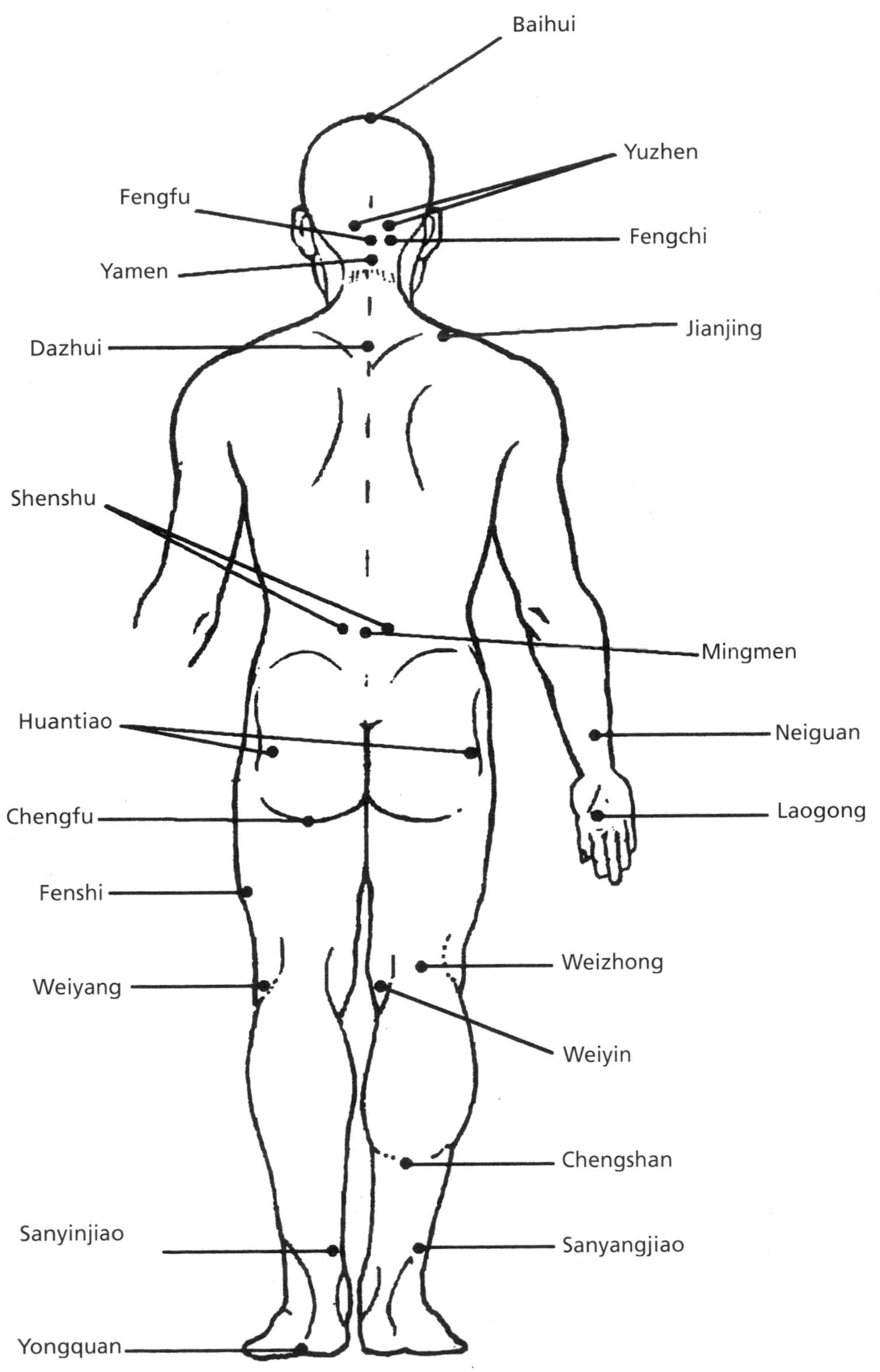
Baihui
Yuzhen
Fengfu
Fengchi
Yamen
Dazhui
Jianjing
Shenshu
Mingmen
Huantiao
Neiguan
Chengfu
Laogong
Fenshi
Weizhong
Weiyang
Weiyin
Chengshan
Sanyinjiao
Sanyangjiao
Yongquan

Every acupuncture point belongs to a channel. Each channel has its own function in relation to the internal organs, nourishing and strengthening them. The acupuncture points keep the channels smooth and ensure that they are working well, bringing in the energy from outside to the body and releasing negative energy out through the skin. In Chinese medicine we say, 'Pain means it is not smooth. Smooth means there is no pain.' This is to do with the channels and acupuncture points working in the body. If you experience pain it means there is a problem. If you don't clear it up, you may become ill.

In China, we have many different ways of keeping the channels smooth and the acupuncture points open. One is massage, which involves person-to-person contact. It manipulates the muscles and acupuncture points, using the hands' Qi or energy to strengthen the organs and to give relief to painful areas. Acupuncturists insert needles into acupuncture points to get rid of the problem and keep the Qi flowing. Moxibustion applies 'burning heat' and medicine to the problem areas and acupuncture points. This heat strengthens the injured areas and brings up the energy. Herbs are used to treat different kinds of problems too. Herbs which grow in the earth belong to nature so they are good for balancing the body.

The last method is Qigong. This is the most effective way, because we ourselves do the exercises that relate to our acupuncture points and channels and build up the Qi to clear the problem. By doing Qigong you build up your resistance to cure the disease. Once it has been cured completely in this way, the Chinese say it will never come back again. Your body will have built up immunity.

3

The Basic Principles of Qigong

'Exercise with energy'

The term Qigong is a combination of two words. The 'Qi' element (sometimes spelt 'Chi', the Cantonese way, or 'Ki', the Japanese way) is usually translated as 'energy'. I think the best way to understand Qi is to look at how the term came about. In Chinese culture rice is very important; today, as in the past, it is still the main ingredient in every meal. When we cook rice we first put it in the pot, then we add water and heat the pot up. After a while you will see steam rising up out of the rice. When the ancient Chinese people first saw this, they called it Qi.

Sky Qi = Weather

Qi is therefore something you can see, something you can smell and something you can feel, but it has no shape and no form. We use the word Qi to describe anything that is related to feelings. For example the weather, which changes all the time and affects our emotions, we call 'sky-Qi'. The air, which we might smell and feel and which also affects our health, we call 'empty-Qi'. We say that people with good morals have 'bone-Qi'. And when you are tired, we say you have 'No spirit and no Qi'. If after a meal at a Chinese restaurant you want to tell them how good the food was, you can say, 'Very good wok-Qi!' Try it – the manager will be very pleased, and you may not have to pay!

Empty Qi = Air

Bone Qi = Morality

No Spirit and No Qi = Tiredness

So the word Qi is used to describe anything relating to 'feeling' or 'energy'. This is why it is so difficult to explain. In the *Dao De Jing*, Lao Zi wrote that Dao cannot be defined – each time you want to

Good Wok Qi = Good Fresh Dishes (of food)

The Chinese character for Qi is made up of the characters for rice and steam.

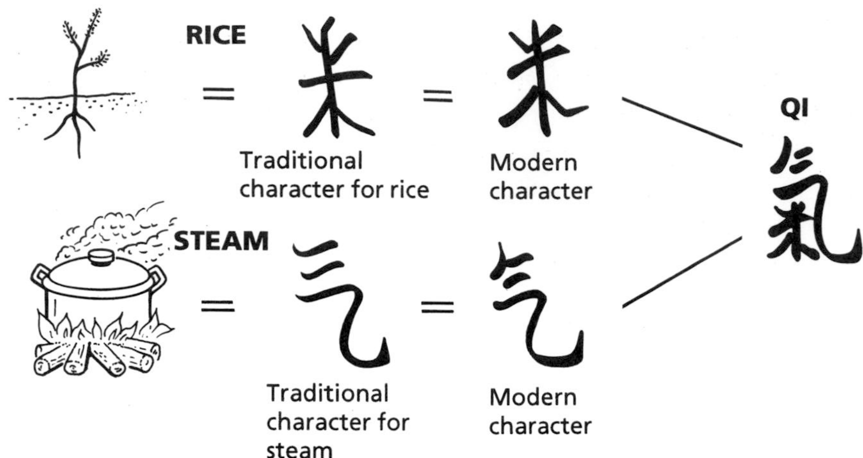

explain it, it has a different meaning. In order to understand it, you need to experience it. Qi is the same: Qi is not just energy, it is more.

If you accept electricity as the embodiment of energy for modern Western society (I call it external energy), you have to accept internal energy – Qi. Qi is the vital energy that maintains our lives; without it we will become tired and ill, and die. External, internal – the principle of Yin and Yang: the one cannot exist without the other to balance it.

The 'gong' part in Qigong means work or exercise. When you go to your office or factory, this is 'gong'. Work with your mind or your strength in this sense is the same as exercise. So Qigong becomes 'exercise with your vital energy'. Some people call it 'Breathing Exercise', 'Longevity Method' or 'Internal Training', but all these names mean the same thing.

Different types of Qigong

There are many, perhaps thousands of kinds of Qigong but normally they are classified into five schools: Daoist, Buddhist, Confucian, medical and martial art. I feel that true Qigong consists only of the Daoist and Buddhist versions. Daoist Qigong concentrates on soft, internal relaxation and steady, gentle training movements with postures moving from soft to hard. Buddhist Qigong is strong, active, dynamic and external in movement with postures moving from hard to soft. Both, however, aim to achieve an equal balance of Yin and

Yang and 'emptiness' of mind. So they are similar and most Qigong follows one of these ways. Confucian Qigong is rare, and the methods are rather basic, indeed simplistic. Medical Qigong is involved with theory, not with practice – it concerns the acupuncture points and channels. Martial art Qigong (such as Taiji Quan, Shaolin Quan, Xing Yi Quan, Bagua Zhang and Wing Chun Kuen) all have their internal training that should not really be considered a separate classification anyway, since any method adopted will belong to either the Daoist or Buddhist schools.

Active and passive Qigong

There are two ways to practise Qigong, one active and the other passive, like Yin and Yang. Active Qigong (Dong Gong) involves movements such as those described in Chapters 8 and 9. The movements relate to our acupuncture points and channels and strengthen the internal organs. Passive Qigong (Jing Gong) consists of any kind of meditation – sitting, lying or standing – which helps us to cultivate energy, storing the Qi in the Dantien. It works on the internal body and clears the mind. Some people also work with visualisation. (See Chapter 10 for more on meditation).

Dantien – the centre

When practising Qigong one part of the body is very important – the centre, known in Chinese as Dantien. It is an area within us that stores our Qi to balance our body – like the sun in our solar system, the father in a family, the capital of a country. 'Dan' means crystal or the essence of energy, while 'Tien' means field or area for the essence of energy. In the beginning when we practise Qigong the Dantien starts to store the Qi energy. At first the Qi stored in the Dantien is gas (air and Qi), which flows around the body causing warm, tingling sensations; then as you progress it becomes liquid, like blood, semen and the milk of a nursing mother. Finally, if you keep practising, the essence of liquid energy becomes crystal (solid) Dan. When high-level Buddhist and Daoist monks die and are cremated, their solid Dan survives and can be found amongst their ashes. Buddhists call this Xie Li Zi.

When we first practise Qigong we bring the Qi to the Dantien (see below). After a while, when the Qi becomes strong enough, it will go through the front channel (Ren Channel) and the back channel (Du

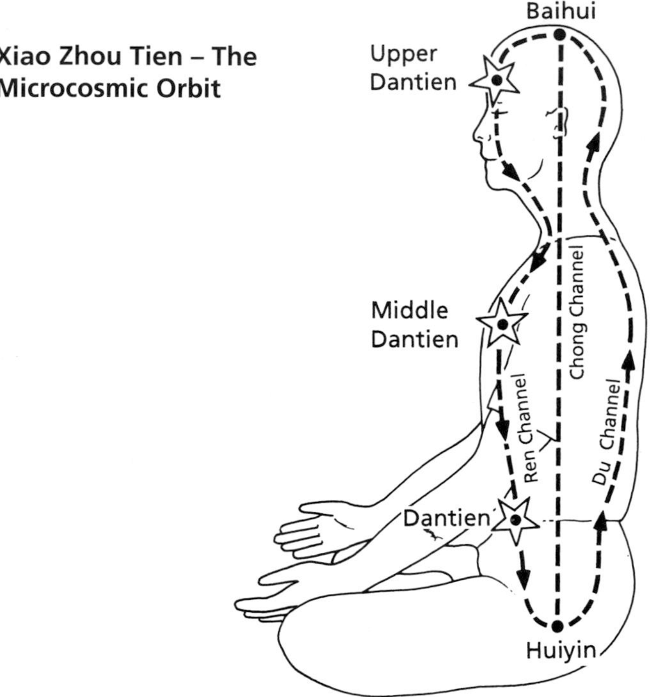

Xiao Zhou Tien – The Microcosmic Orbit

Channel) to form a circle (Xiao Zhou Tien – microcosmic orbit). After this has happened, the twelve main channels will become clear. These are: the Lung Channel; the Pericardium Channel; the Heart Channel; the Spleen Channel; the Liver Channel; the Kidney Channel; the Large Intestine Channel; the Triple Warmer Channel; the Small Intestine Channel; the Stomach Channel; the Gall Bladder Channel; and the Urinary Bladder Channel.

The Dantien is like a bank account: once you have opened it you can put your money in, and the more money you have the more you can deposit. In Qigong, the more energy you collect, the more you can put into your Dantien, so you become healthy and strong (see Chapter 4).

Now we will look at different kinds of training within Qigong. All are aimed at developing your health by collecting Qi and bringing it to the Dantien.

Mind training

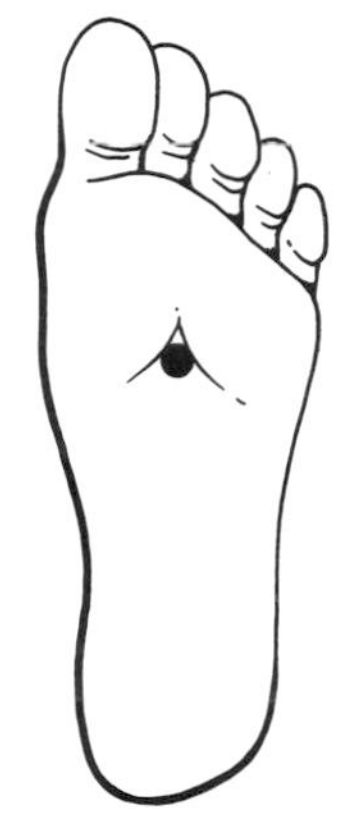
Yongquan point

This training deals with our thoughts. When practising Qigong, the mind is very important. You should not be thinking of other things, but should concentrate on what you are doing. This is particularly important during meditation, when you should be concentrating on your Dantien to ensure that the Qi will be stored there. However, this can be difficult for the beginner. You may find yourself easily distracted by your thoughts. If this is the case, start off by just concentrating on relaxing and then slowly bring your mind to the Dantien.

Some Qigong exercises require you to concentrate on special areas of the body – for example on the Yongquan point, an acupuncture point on the sole of your foot. This point is connected to your kidneys and can benefit hypertension and kidney disease. Other exercises might concentrate on the Laogong point, the acupuncture point on the palm, which is related to the heart, circulation and to releasing negative Qi. Some might concentrate on the Shangzhong point for the heart and lungs. The main thing is always to make sure that your mind is clear and calm during your practice; slowly come to concentration and aim eventually to achieve 'emptiness of mind' when you can become one with the universe, when 'heaven and man become one'. Remember that any direction of Qi through the mind could easily cause a problem which would then be hard to get rid of.

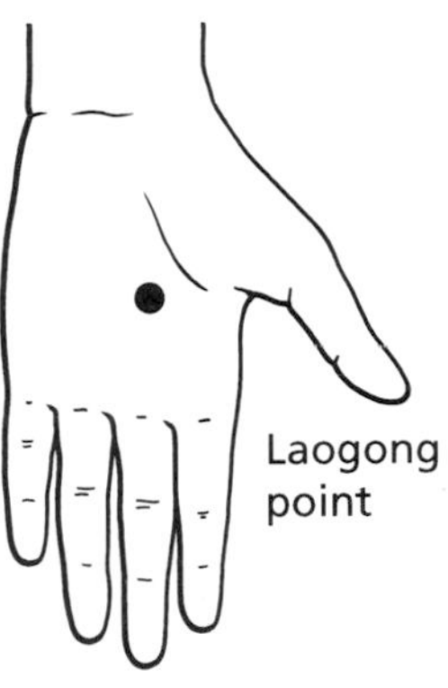
Laogong point

Breathing training

This is another very important part of Qigong, whether you are doing movement or meditation. Your breathing should be in time with your movements. Inhaling brings the positive Qi to your body and is usually accompanied with an 'opening' movement, while exhaling releases the negative Qi and accompanies a 'closing'. In doing so, we increase the strength of the breathing. And we do not breathe just with our lungs – by combining breathing with movement we can collect the energy through the skin, via the acupuncture points. For many people, breathing with the whole body will be a very new experience.

There are movements other than opening and closing. In general, with rising Qigong movements we inhale and with sinking movements we exhale, whereas movements to the left or right may be done with either.

There are also different ways to breathe, as described below. Whichever kind of breathing you use, don't go too far – take it step by step with natural breathing, then use normal or reverse breathing for certain purposes. In fact, if you can relax enough and just practise and forget the way you breathe, unconsciously your breathing will incorporate both normal and reverse breathing.

NATURAL BREATHING

Beginners should use what is called natural breathing. When practising, the breathing should follow your body's movements or feelings and you should not be aware of your breathing – just breathe naturally. Natural breathing is also used during meditation.

NORMAL BREATHING

When you breathe in using this method your abdomen expands, and when you breathe out it contracts. This method is connected with the Dantien, which, as mentioned before, is located in the area below the navel. Thus the expanding and contracting of the abdomen stimulates the Dantien.

REVERSE BREATHING

Reverse breathing is the opposite of normal breathing. When you inhale the abdomen contracts, and when you exhale the abdomen expands. This method of breathing is actually stronger and a slightly higher level of practice, because it makes the Dantien stronger and stimulates the Ren (front) and Du (back) channels. However, do not think that just because it is a higher level you should use it all the time. It is like sweets – one or two are nice, but if you eat too many you will get stomach ache and lose your appetite or your teeth. Reverse breathing creates fire in your body. We only use it at certain times and for a short while, particularly during meditation (perform it either twelve or twenty-four times only, inhaling and exhaling being counted as one).

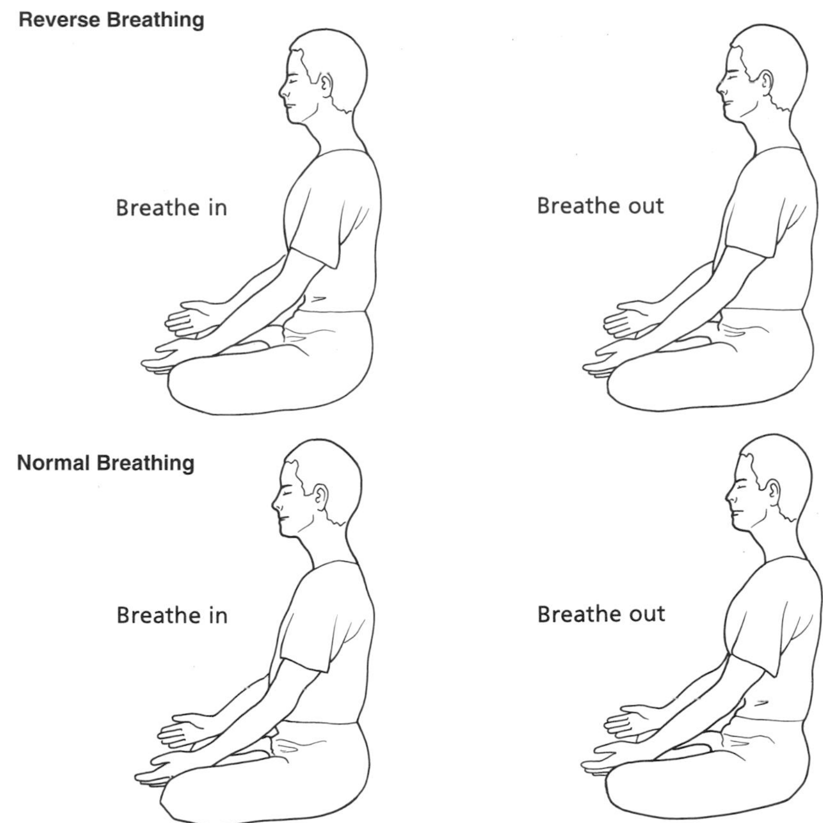

Body training

By 'body' we mean posture and movement, and these are very important. If we just concentrate on the mind and do not concern ourselves with movement and posture, we are not doing Qigong.

In Qigong practice your back should be straight so that the Baihui point or Sky-door (on the top of the head) and the Huiyin point (between the legs near the anus) are in line and vertical. This posture allows you to gather the 'heaven' and 'earth' Qi and allows your Qi to flow naturally. You don't lose too much energy and so you won't get tired easily. Bending forwards or backwards suppresses the lungs, causes the breath to be short and results in your losing Qi. Keeping the mouth closed lets the Qi flow down to the Dantien. It also allows the negative Qi to sink down through the legs and release out to the earth. This lets the positive Qi rise up to the lungs, heart, forehead and Baihui point.

The area between the Baihui point and the forehead is connected with the brain and known as the Upper Dantien (see page 30). On the forehead is an acupuncture point known as the Sky-eye or Yintang point, which helps to calm the brain and gathers fresh Qi.

Relaxing all the joints helps the Qi pass through the entire body – just like keeping the motorways clear allows people to travel to different parts of the country. Relaxing the joints allows more Qi to go to the organs and allows negative Qi around a problem area to be released. And, of course, it allows the blood to circulate, which keeps the blood pressure normal.

There are a number of other elements to be taken into consideration. For example, sometimes we need to close the eyes or squeeze the toes, lift up the anus, keep the head upright or bend slightly forwards, keep your weight on the left or the right, and so on. All these movements are used in different exercises under different circumstances. But the important thing is to relax your mind and your body, which will allow everything inside you to work naturally and easily.

Practice

Daily practice is extremely important. It is just like brushing your teeth – it should become a routine activity that you never miss. Many people, however, buy a lot of books or attend classes, but they never practise regularly at home and thus do not feel the full benefit.

Practising Qigong is the way to apply all the knowledge you have gained and to experience how Qigong and Qi can help you.

After reading this book, make a timetable for your practice. In the first week, start off with just three exercises and add another three the next week and so on. In just four weeks you can complete the movements of Balancing Gong and, in another six, you can complete the Taiji Qigong sequence.

An important point to remember when practising is that when you have finished your active Qigong, you should choose a meditation to do during which you can gather Qi. Active Qigong opens the channels and meditation collects the Qi at the Dantien. So Yang goes to Yin.

For more information on practising Qigong, see Chapter 7.

4

The Benefits of Qigong Practice

Youthfulness

People have frequently tried to guess my age and got it wrong. Many of them think that I am five, seven, even ten years younger than I am. This makes me feel very pleased (who doesn't want others to think they are younger than they actually are?). It's all a result of my daily Qigong practice.

First, Qigong makes my body strong and healthy. I have more energy for everyday life, because Qigong follows the natural way to strengthen the internal body. Based on Chinese medicine, Yin and Yang, the acupuncture points and channels, and concentrating on the breathing, mind and movement, Qigong brings the body back to normal, working with nature to follow the universal rhythm.

After a couple of months' practice your body will change noticeably and you will become stronger and healthier. When you are healthy your face will change. Your expression will contain more energy and your eyes will show more spirit, and so you will look younger. The condition of your skin improves as more natural oils are produced to nourish it. Even without creams and cosmetics your face will have a better colour and become smoother and softer.

Return to a healthy size and shape

Not only will you look younger, but your whole body will go back to normal. For example, if you are naturally thin and have become overweight, you will become thin again. If you are naturally big you will become big again. But you will still be healthy. It all depends on what size you inherited from your parents. If you are thin and suddenly become fat, that means you are not natural, not balanced, and so you will be ill. The same will happen if you are naturally fat and try to make yourself thin. A big tree is big and a small tree is small! Everything has its own rhythm, its own way.

After many years practising Qigong my size is the same as it was when I was a young adult – not too fat and not too thin. Within Qigong practice there are many movements that exercise the joints and the waist. They help the circulation through the body and any excess fat is released. So do not worry – you won't become too fat!

In some thin people, the internal organs may be weak and not functioning as well as they should. For example, a small chest means small lungs and heart, and if people have small hips it means their kidneys are weak. Through Qigong you can make these parts strong and they will become their correct size.

Improved posture and attitude

Because Qigong trains your body, skeleton and breathing, it automatically corrects your posture: your back will be straight, chest up, shoulders relaxed and waist flexible. With correct posture you will look taller and stronger.

Some very tall people adopt a stooping posture which makes them tired and weak. They lack confidence, so they look smaller. In contrast, someone who is small but has a healthy posture, the right skeleton and the correct balance between body and limbs looks taller and more confident. A healthy body means that the internal organs are healthy. You will not become bad-tempered, angry, over-excited or depressed – all these emotions are affected by your internal balance. A good, healthy body brings a good attitude, while a bad, unhealthy body brings a bad attitude. The mind and body are undeniably connected.

Problem-solving via meditation

Meditation can help you to solve your problems. You may find, for instance, that when you are at work and need to make a difficult decision you just do not know what to do. Meditation can help you find the best answer, because it enables you to cast off all the stress and pressure of the situation so that your mind has more room to move and you can see the problem more clearly. We often panic, especially if we have lost something, and because we are too close to the question we cannot see the answer. Stay away and forget it; then the solution will come naturally.

More energy, less stress

When your body becomes healthy, you will find you have more energy and do not tire so easily. You become aware of your body's condition and of when you are pushing yourself too hard. So you never suffer from work-related stress because you know when you are over-exerting yourself. When you lose the ability to judge your body's condition, you can easily become ill or suffer from chronic conditions like ME, heart disease and even cancer. When the body is exhausted it loses its ability to release the negative and gather the positive Qi.

A positive approach to life

Through practising Qigong you do not just become physically healthy, but your mind and your emotions also become more stable. The Chinese say, 'Anything that happens on the inside shows on the outside.' We cannot hide ourselves by *acting* healthy and positive, because our real condition will always reveal itself. So the best thing to do is improve your health and achieve balance with nature.

I have seen many people who were ill and depressed, but then started doing Qigong and changed dramatically. Day by day they became more confident, more positive, more sociable and better equipped to deal with life's changes and situations. So no matter how clever, how well educated or even wealthy you are, remember that you need a healthy body to carry your talents and your character.

Greater opportunities

When you look healthy and positive, people are naturally attracted to you and like being close to you. With more people around you, you find that you have more opportunities both at work and socially. Many people feel that they endure a lot of bad luck, but it is actually their health that is affecting their lives. Being unhealthy affects your emotions and your balance, which makes you appear negative and so others naturally avoid you. Just your appearance can change the way people treat you. Don't miss out on the opportunities that healthy people get: it is your health that brings you luck.

Better brainpower, better judgement

Qigong optimises the functioning power of the brain, improving your memory and attention to detail. You will find that you are better able to cope with difficult subjects or skills that previously were a real struggle.

When you practise Qigong you will become much more calm and relaxed, and when you are 'open' in this way you are in a far better position to judge whether a situation or person is good or bad for you. For example, when you first meet someone, you will immediately be able to tell whether to trust him or not. You are not so easily impressed by the way he talks or the way he dresses and so you are able to sense his character – his heart. When you come to a new place, you can tell whether it is good for you – a good place to work or a good place to stay; you could even sense danger before it happens.

We humans still have something in common with animals – we can sense our environment and imminent problems. Qigong brings us back to nature, enabling us to stay away from what is artificial and letting the natural senses return.

Healing specific ailments

As I have already mentioned, Qigong can be used not just for improving health but also for self-healing. The chart opposite will help you to pinpoint the exercises that are especially good for some common everyday ailments. If you wish to work with a particular condition, you should concentrate on the exercises recommended for its treatment. For more serious complaints, it is best to seek advice from your therapist as different exercises will be recommended for different individuals.

Qigong for Self-Healing

AILMENT	EXERCISE
Arthritis	Big Bear Stretches *73* Taiji Start *82* Marching While Bouncing the Ball *117*
Asthma	Roc Extends its Wings *74* Opening the Chest *84* Pushing the Wave *112*
Backache	Beautiful Woman Turns Her Waist *70* Rowing the Boat in the Middle of the Lake *94* Rotating the Wheel in a Circle *110* *and see page 40*
Bad circulation	Cloud Steps *78* Separating the Clouds *92* Flying Pigeon *115* Looking at the Sky, Touching the Sea *116*
Co-ordination	Rolling the Arms *89* Cloud Hands in Horse Stance *103* Marching While Bouncing the Ball *117*
Constipation	Holding the Dantien *62* The Dantien: Up and Down *64* Opening and Closing the Dantien *66* Punching *106*
Convalescence	Flying Wild Goose *109* Holding the Dantien *62* The Dantien: Up and Down *64* Opening and Closing the Dantien *66* Taiji Start *82* Separating the Clouds *92*
Depression	Big Bear Stretches *73* Supporting the Sky *76* Opening the Chest *84* *and see page 40*
Fatigue	Cloud Steps *78* Flying Wild Goose *109* Pushing the Wave *112*
Headache	Cloud Steps *78* Rainbow Dance *86* Rolling the Arms *89* Looking at the Sky, Touching the Sea *116*
Insomnia	Holding the Dantien *62* The Dantien: Up and Down *64* Opening and Closing the Dantien *66* Cloud Steps *78* Cloud Hands in Horse Stance *103* Marching While Bouncing the Ball *117*
Kidney problems	Beautiful Woman Turns Her Waist *70* Rowing the Boat in the Middle of the Lake *94* Turning the Body to Look at the Moon *98* Turning Waist to Pushing Palm *100* Rotating the Wheel in a Circle *110*
Neck problems	Turning the Head and Twisting the Tail *69* Peeping Monkey *71* Monkey Walk *80* Rolling the Arms *89* Lifting Up the Ball *96*
Nervous disorders	Turning the Head and Twisting the Tail *69* Cloud Steps *78* Lifting Up the Ball *96*
M.E.	Cloud Steps *78* Opening the Chest *84* Rowing the Boat in the Middle of the Lake *94* Punching *106*
Slimming	Roc Extends its Wings *74* Lifting Up the Ball *96* Turning the Body to Look at the Moon *98* Punching *106* Rotating the Wheel in a Circle *110*
Stomach ache	Beautiful Woman Turns Her Waist *70* Rainbow Dance *86* Separating the Clouds *92* Rowing the Boat in the Middle of the Lake *94*

The page references in italics show you where to find each exercise

Here are a couple of quick and easy remedies for two common complaints – backache and depression. Try them!

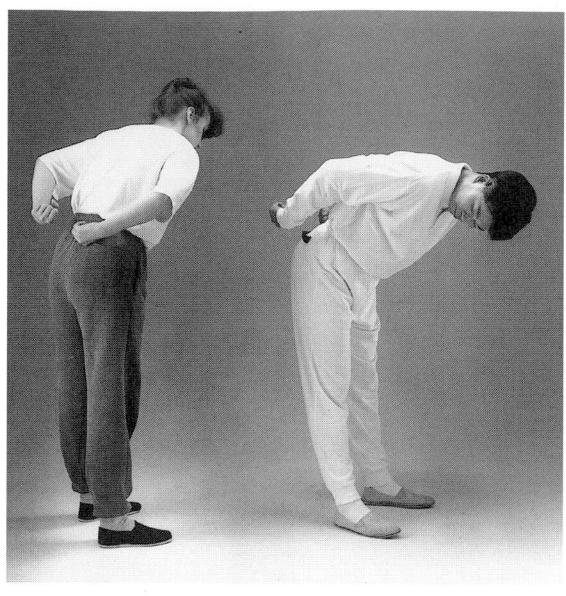

Curing backache

1.◂ Lean forwards and pummel your lower back with your fists.

Alleviating depression

1.▾◂ Place the right hand on the left side of the chest while placing your left on your back.

2.▾ Move your right hand in a downwards stroke to finish at your waist. Breathe in as you do so.

Repeat several times.

5

Postnatal and Prenatal Qi

The secret energy users

EATING AND DRINKING

Before we start, perhaps I should explain that the terms I use in the chapter title have nothing whatsoever to do with having babies – they refer to different kinds of energy! . . . If you were to ask a friend or work colleague, 'How do you get the energy that you need to live?', assuming of course that he was an 'ordinary' person who knew nothing about health exercises and Qigong, he would answer, 'From eating and drinking.'

That's the right answer – for the ordinary person. Of course without food you will die within about twenty days and without water in a much shorter time. So eating and drinking are very important for everyone. But did you know that we pay a price for eating and drinking? I don't mean in terms of money, but in terms of energy.

Have you noticed that after a meal you often feel tired and sleepy? This is because most of the energy in your body goes to your stomach to digest the food. As a result your brain loses energy, your mind is not as clear, and you feel sleepy. The same is true of what we drink. Only pure water is absorbed directly; from other liquids, such as supermarket soft drinks and alcohol, the body has to separate out the beneficial elements and eliminate the negative ones. Even something healthy like fresh fruit juice cannot be absorbed directly to become part of us. So whenever we eat or drink, we need to use our energy – our Qi.

BREATHING

Take another case – breathing. Now breathing is a very important way of getting energy. Indeed, if you stop breathing for just a couple of minutes you will die. But it too can 'cost energy' because your body has to separate out the good from the bad. Of course, if you are in the countryside surrounded by trees and mountains, by a river or on a grassy plain with just the sky above, the pure fresh air you inhale will not cost you anything in energy terms. But most people live or work in cities which are polluted, for instance by cars emitting carbon monoxide into the atmosphere. Factories and offices contain machines and air conditioning systems which release a lot of heat and negative air. Even at home we are surrounded by electricity cables, computers, televisions, radios and cigarette smoke.

All this radiation, carbon monoxide and other 'artificial elements' around us damages our bodies. But this is the air or energy that we inhale into our lungs and which is stored in our kidneys. In Chinese medicine we say that the lungs inhale the energy, while the kidneys store the energy. Those elements from the air we breathe which enter our bloodstream stay in our liver, because the liver stores blood and helps to transfer it, with its nutritional contents, to the other organs and the brain as well. So the bad air we breathe damages the entire body, not just one part. This is a different concept from that of Western medicine. In Chinese medicine the whole body is interconnected and everything must be balanced.

So if we take negative air into the body, the kidneys have to work on it to eliminate the negative parts and pass them out, as do the lungs and the skin. And all this work needs to use energy. So if we are in a place that does not have enough fresh air, it will make us tired. A lot of elderly people like to stay at home, particularly in the winter; they are afraid of the cold. So they keep the heating on and the windows shut, burning the oxygen out of the air. Then they fall asleep. As a result they find themselves getting even more tired and weak. But they think this is just a normal condition of old age. Even doctors tell them, 'Oh, that's only to be expected at your age. Just get more rest and you will be all right.' But basically what they are missing is the main source of energy – fresh air! The best thing to do is to open windows for a couple of minutes in the morning and evening to allow the house to breathe. You may even save on your heating bill because fresh air warms up more quickly than stale air!

SLEEP

Every night we come home after a hard day at work or after socialising with friends and feel tired. We think sleep can recharge our energy, and so we go to bed. Yes, sleep is rest – and without enough sleep you will become ill. But did you know that sleep too uses up energy?

Sometimes when you wake up in the morning you will still feel tired and sleepy. This is because there is a right and a wrong way to sleep, and you have picked the wrong way. If at night you just lie down on your bed without any preparation, you are not sleeping – you are collapsing! And when you lie down and close your eyes it does not necessarily mean you are resting. Your brain is still working, thinking, creating pictures and the images of your dreams, and you are still using energy.

However, if you meditate before going to bed, you will be in a relaxed state. In meditation there are two kinds of images created by the mind. The first will take our energy and affect our state of calmness and balance; these are called distracting thoughts, for example thoughts about your work, your family, your plans etc. The others come naturally, and you might see pictures of trees, flowers, people and so on that make you feel peaceful and relaxed. Spontaneous thoughts of this kind will help your mind and your energy to develop.

Further energy can be wasted through bad posture when sleeping. If your body is in the wrong position some of the channels or veins will be blocked, causing poor circulation. Your dreams may become very strange and even nightmarish. When you wake up in the middle of the night you might find that your hands are on your chest, putting pressure on your heart, or maybe that you have been sleeping on your side in a posture that compressed the lungs, causing a breathing problem. So some sleeping positions cause problems for your energy flow, and the following day you will feel tired and stiff in your neck, back or shoulders. Your energy will always go to any part of the body that is blocked or suppressed, to try to bring it back to normal. The best sleeping posture is lying on your back with a pillow to support your head, legs slightly apart and arms loosely by your side, i.e. a similar position to that used in lying meditation.

When you want to go to sleep you need to prepare your mind and body. Take some fresh air, or just close your eyes for a while. The best preparation is a combination of Qigong and meditation. This will allow you to have a good night's sleep and wake up refreshed, because your body and mind will be balanced and this will reveal your body's true condition. When you practise Qigong regularly, it may well enable you to tell whether you are tired and need to sleep or if you are still in strong spirit.

Postnatal Qi

The energy we get from eating, drinking, sleeping and breathing – and you now know how to optimise the energy acquired in these ways – is known as Postnatal Qi. The ancient text known as *The Yellow Emperor's Canon of Internal Medicine* mentions the Jing of water and grain – Jing is sexual energy or gene energy. Breathing and sleeping we designate as Qi from the air.

Postnatal Qi is the energy that comes to you, as its name suggests, after you are born. You need this energy to maintain your life – like a seed in the ground, which needs light and water otherwise the plant will not grow.

To acquire Postnatal Qi we need to work – in other words, we need to use energy in order to get more energy. When you cannot afford any more energy you will become ill and have to rely on other things – medicines from the West or East, acupuncture, herbal remedies, massage and so on. And when these can no longer help, you will have come to the end of life's road.

Prenatal Qi

There is, however, another kind of energy that you will not have used up even at this stage. Prenatal Qi or True Qi, which is hidden in the centre of your body, the Dantien, comes from your parents (see also Chapter 4).

The Yellow Emperor's Canon of Internal Medicine describes in its first chapter our Original Qi or True Qi. We grow up from our parents' Qi – Yang which comes from the father, Yin from the mother.

Yin and Yang Qi come together, become one and create another Qi. This is True Qi (Original or Prenatal Qi), which will grow every day by absorbing Postnatal Qi like food, water, air and sleep. This True Qi from your parents is like a seed. A seed needs to take nutrients from the soil, air, water and sunlight (in other words, Postnatal Qi)

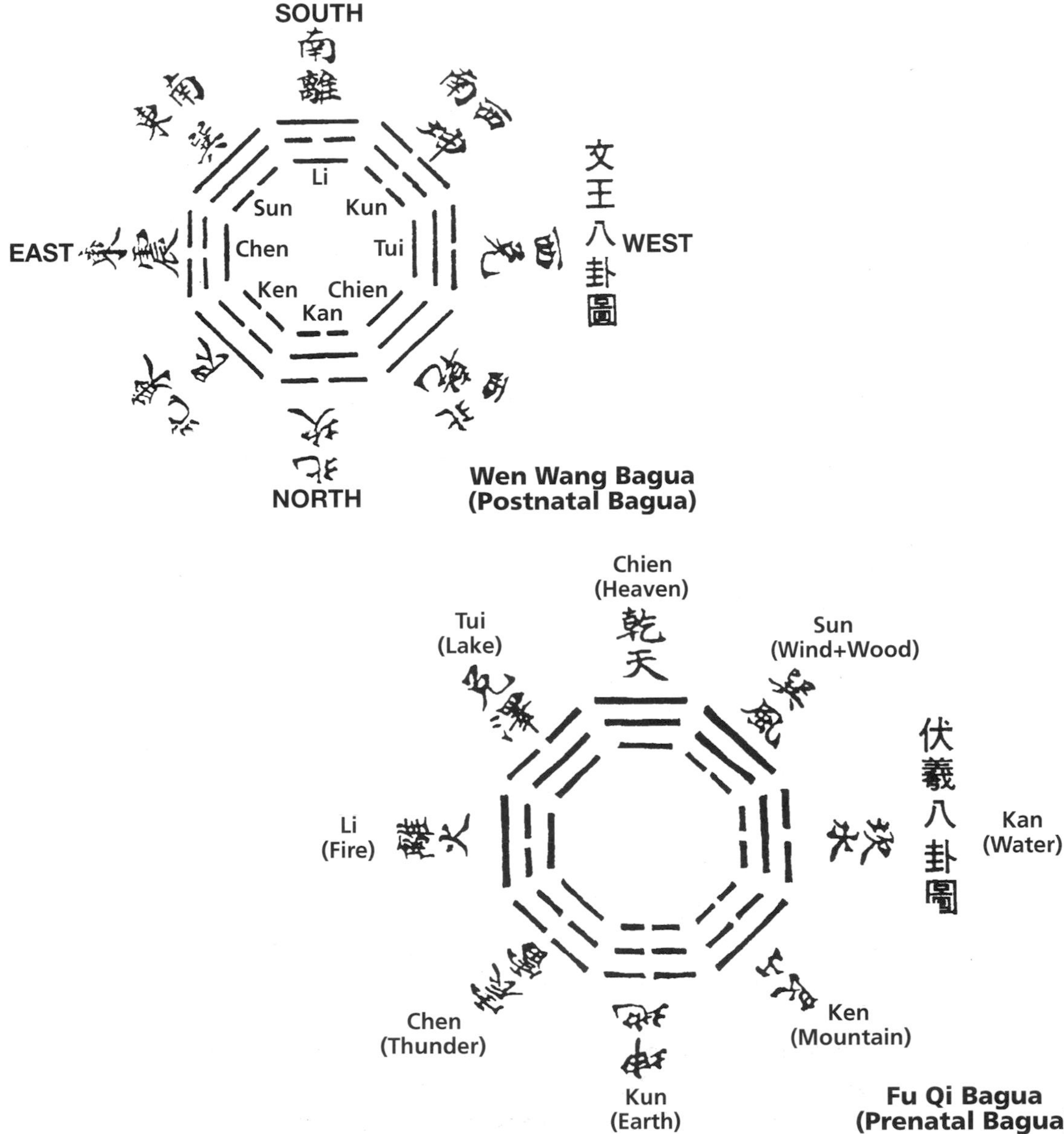

to grow into a big tree. But to do so, this small seed must contain powerful Prenatal energy.

Basically, whether you are strong or weak, healthy or unhealthy, depends on your Original Qi – whether your parents gave you a healthy body with strong internal organs and a strong skeleton.

FEMALE ENERGY THROUGHOUT LIFE

The *Huangdi Neijing* says female energy takes seven years for each stage of development. Normally when a girl reaches the age of seven her kidneys start to develop and so her teeth begin to change and her hair grows. This is all because her Original Qi (which is stored at the centre of the body and is related to the kidneys) starts to 'work'.

When she reaches fourteen, her Tin Kwai begins to develop. This is our generative power, for having babies and sex. The Ren (front) Channel and Chong Channel (the centre channel, inside the body) become strong, to allow the womb to develop. So her menstruation starts and she can have babies.

At twenty-one, her kidneys are strong and the wisdom teeth grow – teeth, hair and kidneys are all connected. They are signs of a person's health and how strong their energy is. She is also fully grown.

At twenty-eight she is fully developed. The body has reached its peak. Hair, muscles, bones and the shape of her body become mature. Also her brain is fully developed and mature.

Coming up to thirty-five, the Yangming Channels (the Large Intestine Channel of Hand Yangming, and the Stomach Channel of Foot Yangming), both of which pass through the face, become weak. So her face begins to look tired and some hair is lost. This means that her energy, having come up to the top, begins to drop back down again, becoming weaker.

At forty-two the three Yang Channels (the Large Intestine Channel of Hand Yangming, the Stomach Channel of Foot Yangming, and the Small Intestine Channel of Hand Taiyang) become weak. This causes the face to dry and the hair to turn grey.

At forty-nine the Ren Channel becomes empty, losing its Qi. The Chong Channel too becomes weak, losing its blood and its Qi. This causes the Tin Kwai to stop, so her menstruation ceases and now she can no longer have babies. Also the body and face start to look old.

MALE ENERGY THROUGHOUT LIFE

For men the changes in their development come every eight years and the development ends later than for women. In a boy of eight the kidneys start to 'work', producing more hair, and the milk teeth change.

At sixteen the Qi of the kidneys becomes strong and so puberty starts, releasing sperm. Thus his Tin Kwai starts to work. The Yin and Yang Qi inside the body become strong and balanced, and from this moment he can father a child.

When he reaches twenty-four his kidneys are very strong. The muscles and skeleton have become stronger, and he now has his wisdom teeth.

At thirty-two the body is fully developed. It reaches its full height, and the muscles and bones are fully developed.

Forty is the time when a man's body begins to run down. The kidney Qi becomes weak, and so he begins to lose hair and teeth.

At forty-eight the Yang Qi in the body becomes weak. Tiredness and greyness show in the face.

At fifty-six the kidneys become weak and this affects the liver. In the Five Elements of Chinese philosophy (see Chapter 4) the kidneys are water and the liver is wood. Water supports wood, and so if water is lost then wood becomes weak. The body then becomes stiff, as the muscles lose their flexibility.

At sixty-four the kidneys have decayed and Tin Kwai stops, so there is no sperm. Many teeth are lost, and a lot of hair. The body has become old.

Daily Qigong practice keeps your channels open and healthy thus slowing down the ageing process. You can continue to enjoy good health and vitality as you grow older.

Achieving balance

When your body comes to balance, your Prenatal Qi will come through. This energy can keep you forever – it lasts throughout your life and can develop your hidden potential.

So how can we come to balance? You have to bring your body to a point between consciousness and unconsciousness, when you are neither awake nor collapsed. By practising Qigong you first reach a level of relaxation, then you come to the balanced state that will open your Prenatal Qi. At first you find your body relaxes. Then you become used to the exercise and you come to a point where you can do the movements without thinking – where you can forget everything, even yourself!

Your whole body becomes quiet and you do not even notice your breathing, which slows down and seems to stop. This means you begin to breathe with your skin, through your acupuncture points. Now your body becomes part of the universe and you can recharge your energy.

You will feel strong sensations flowing down the Front (Ren) Channel, through the Huiyin point (the acupuncture point between the two legs) and then going up through the Back (Du) Channel. The sensation may be warm and tingling, and you might see colours around your body and fingers. Whatever sensations you feel, treat them as normal. The main thing is that you are in the balanced state, whether you are meditating or performing movement; this will promote your Prenatal Qi.

THE EFFECTS OF DEVELOPING YOUR PRENATAL QI

When your Prenatal Qi has developed, you might see the colours of Qi: red, green, yellow, black, purple, and so on, just as mentioned before about the original image of Qi. It is something that you might feel, smell or see. The colours you see, basically, come from the five major organs in the body: red comes from the heart, green from the liver, yellow from the spleen and black or purple from the kidneys. Other organs such as the stomach, intestines, gall bladder and so on are connected to those five. You will see colour either in the skin of yourself or another, or in the energy field surrounding a person, which Westerners call the 'aura'.

When your Prenatal Qi becomes very highly developed you may be able to heal others (see Chapter 6). But always remember that however our potential and energy come out, they must develop naturally. The Chinese say, 'Follow nature and live. Go against nature and you will be eliminated.' When your potential develops, take it easy. Being healthy is the most important thing of all.

6

Healing Others with Highly Developed Qi

Transmitting Qi

When their Prenatal Qi develops, some people have strong Qi and can heal others. For example, if one of your friends were suffering from a stomach ache or a shoulder strain, you would just touch them where the pain was and suddenly they would find that the pain had gone and they felt much more relaxed. This is because you transmitted your Qi to the blocked area of your friend's body, smoothing the channels and releasing the negative energy. You become, in effect, an acupuncturist who does not use needles. This is how I work with my patients. If your Qi is strong enough you can transmit it to people at a distance, you do not need to touch the person to heal them.

Heightened receptivity

Sometimes, when you are at home and find yourself thinking of a close friend, suddenly he rings you and you suppose it must be coincidental. Or maybe you are talking with your friend and are both thinking the same – even wanting to speak at the same time. All these things can happen because your Prenatal Qi has developed and areas on the upper part of your head, which we call Sky-eye and Sky-door (acupuncture points on the head), have opened, so that you can receive messages from outside. You know what other people are thinking and doing even when they are far away from you.

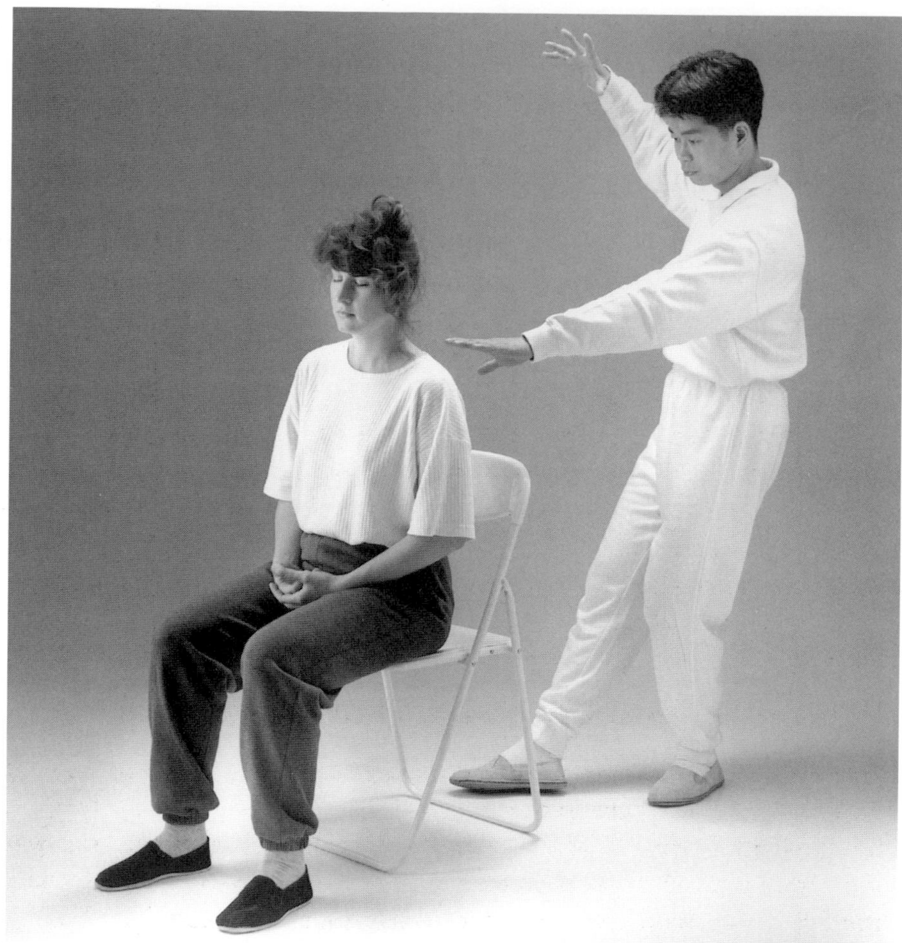

Michael demonstrating the technique of Qi transmission.

The importance of self-healing in healing others

People in the West have a tendency to home in on the techniques and to gloss over the importance of the energy, the Qi, which is the essential element in the process. Healers are constantly giving their Qi to others during the healing process, and so they must constantly recharge their own Qi through Qigong practice. If you are attempting to heal others, and are not yourself healthy through practising the movements and meditation of Qigong, you will transmit negative rather than positive Qi – which must, of course, be avoided. If, for example, your patient had a back problem and after treatment finds their heart beating faster, you could well have passed a heart problem of your own on to the patient.

Healing is a mutual commitment

One of my patients, Sophie D., was suffering from breast cancer. She came to see me because she has more faith in Chinese medicine than in Western medicine; also she had seen my Qigong demonstrations and attended some of my seminars. After five treatments her condition had improved considerably – not just because my Qi cured her, but because she followed my instructions and every day did the exercises I had given her. Then one of the lumps disappeared. I believe that one day she will totally recover just by keeping up with the exercises.

Qigong therapy does not just rely on the therapist – it also needs the patient's co-operation, otherwise it will not work. Therapist and patient must work together to improve the condition.

Further examples of healing with Qi

Jean K. had suffered from the utterly debilitating condition of myalgic encephalomyelitis (also known as ME or post-viral syndrome) for many years. Then one of my students introduced her to me, and after five treatments she was able to go back to her studies and her job at the BBC. She said that during the treatments she could feel my Qi running through her body, making her feel warm and comfortable. Afterwards she felt more energetic and much stronger.

She also benefited from the exercises and meditation that I taught her. Qigong is especially effective in treating chronic and debilitating conditions such as ME as it boosts your energy levels. This is because during practice your body enters an energy storing phase, similar to that experienced when you are very relaxed or asleep. Oxygen consumption drops and the metabolic rate decreases so that if you remain in this phase for a reasonable length of time while still awake, you stop the loss of energy from your body and facilitate the storage of the fresh energy obtained by your body.

Jo C. suffered from backache and had no feeling in her legs, particularly in her feet. She could not feel what she was walking on, and had many times scalded her feet by unknowingly putting them into water that was too hot. For two years she had not worked and had been unable to go out. Then someone introduced her to me. After three months of treatment she went back to work, and her back had become much stronger. Although she still has no feeling in her feet, she finds life much easier.

The importance of conserving energy

During these treatments, I used my Qi to make my patients' energy stronger, to get rid of negative Qi, to smooth the channels, to open the acupuncture points and to strengthen the internal organs. When the internal organs achieve balance, the illness goes. But after the treatment the patient needs to conserve his or her energy. No matter how famous the Qigong master who uses his energy to help you, if you do not keep the energy but use it to enjoy your life, playing games, chatting with your friends or watching TV, you will become exhausted and will regress to how you were before your treatment.

After treatment I teach my patients special exercises and meditation for their particular condition. During treatment I use my own energy to help them, and afterwards they practise Qigong exercises at home and create energy equal to that given in the treatments, so that they do not need me any more. The problem diminishes as their energy gets stronger, and in the end it is eliminated. In this way the illness is cured and immunity is built up so it will not recur. This is the best part of Qigong practice and also the best kind of treatment to give any sick person, as it has no side-effects.

PART TWO

Qigong Exercises

7

Before You Start

In Chapters 8 and 9 I describe in detail how to do certain Qigong exercises, but first I want to cover one or two general points.

When to practise

Throughout this book I have explained how important it is to do your Qigong practice on a regular, daily basis. Do this in a relaxed way and your body will gradually lead you on the path to good health.

You can do your practice at any time of day, but because people today lead such busy lives you might find it simplest to do a session first thing in the morning and another in the evening before you go to bed. In that way you will set up a routine, so you are less likely to forget your practice or find that other activities are competing for the same time-slot. Twenty minutes twice a day is enough to bring up your Qi level. But if you have the time and enjoy doing your Qigong exercises there is no reason why you should not extend your practice to half an hour, or even an hour – there is no risk involved, and you will then definitely become healthy! On the other hand if you only have five or ten minutes to spare, you can still benefit.

THE ZI TIME AND THE MAO TIME

Although Qigong can be performed at any hour of the day, really keen practitioners choose what are known as the Zi time (11 p.m. to 1 a.m.) and the Mao time (5 a.m. to 7 a.m.). These times relate to the liver and lungs; the liver is connected to the blood and its circulation, while the lungs connect to the breathing and Qi.

What to practise

Earlier in the book I suggested that to begin with you could work your way through the Balancing Gong and Taiji Qigong sequences, learning several exercises a week, until you are familiar with all the movements. Once you are familiar with them, however, you may wish to pick and choose which exercises to include in each practice. You don't need to stick to the sequences or do the exercises in any particular order. You can simply practise the exercises you feel you need or the ones that appeal to you. You will probably find that the ones you like are the ones you need anyway! Each exercise can be repeated as you wish. The Chinese like to do things in multiples of six – so you could, for example, repeat an exercise six, twelve or twenty-four times.

The right direction to face

The four points of the compass relate to different internal organs: East for the liver, West for the lungs, North for the kidneys and South for the heart. If you have a health problem in any of these areas, face the appropriate direction. If, however, you have a problem with your stomach, you can face whichever direction you like – this is because the stomach is the centre.

But our health problems are also connected to our Yin and Yang, and you might find that you need to face the opposite direction from those indicated above. Too much Yang means we have too much energy, and conversely too much Yin indicates that our energy is weak. For example, if you have a bad temper because of bad circulation, it means that your liver is too Yang. Therefore you should face West (the opposite of the normal direction for liver complaints) to release your excess liver Qi.

Feelings during Qigong practice

Normally when you practise Qigong you will experience sensations of warmth, tingling, itchiness and electricity. Whatever you feel, just let it happen – the feelings will find their own way to balance you.

Sometimes, however, you may feel sleepy; this means that you are tired and should rest. Alternatively you might feel cold or even in pain. This means that you have a problem in the area where you are experiencing pain because the Qi is not flowing well there, and you need to practise more.

Warnings and health restrictions

Qigong deals with the internal body and mind which is full of Qi and which must follow 'the natural way'. Any artificial ways are not good for your Qi, so during practice you must make sure you relax the body and calm the mind. Alcohol, smoking and medicines will affect you – you may feel sick, dizzy, tired or weak. You should try and avoid practising if you are feeling any extremes of emotion, for instance if you feel very sad, angry or worried. Try also to practise away from any source of pollution – traffic or other fumes, radiation (turn off the television and radio), and excess noise as this will harm and shock your body, damaging the rhythm and flow of Qi. If you find yourself being distracted during practice, it is best to stop doing the exercise, complete with Shou Gong (see page 118) and find another time or place to continue.

There are no physical health problems for which it is inadvisable to practise Qigong, so long as you relax while you do your practice and do things at your own natural pace.

MENSTRUATION

There are no restrictions for women practising Qigong during menstruation. Practising Qigong can help your circulation during a period and so ease headaches, stomach cramps and any emotional problems. This is because during menstruation the body changes due to the change in the blood circulation and pressure, and by practising Qigong you can calm and balance the blood.

Some women, however, have very heavy periods. If this is the case, you should change your meditation so that instead of concentrating on the Dantien, you concentrate on the middle Dantien – the Shanzhong point. This is because the Dantien is related to the womb area and concentration on it may over-stimulate the area during a period, making it even heavier. It is better to move your concentration to the higher Shanzhong point which is related to the heart and lungs.

PREGNANCY

Qigong can still be practised during pregnancy, but you should take care while bending and doing very active movements. Take things gently and be aware of the effects of the movements on your body. Meditation is very beneficial during pregnancy as you can connect with your baby, giving it strong Qi which helps to promote good health and intelligence and enables you to form strong bonds which will be very valuable for you both in the future.

Comfort

It is important to find a quiet and peaceful environment, either indoors or outdoors, in which to practise. Make sure you have plenty of fresh air but do not practise in a draught. Wear clothes that are loose and comfortable. During a lying meditation you may wish to cover yourself with a light blanket to avoid becoming cold.

It is best not to practise Qigong on either an empty or a full stomach. Wait for at least thirty minutes after eating.

Taking part in other sports: pros and cons

People who are starting to practise Qigong often ask if it is all right to participate in other sports such as swimming, football, tennis, weight training and so on. There is no reason why you should not continue to enjoy these activities, but you will of course be using up the Qi that you have stored. This is because fitness training in the West is based on the principle of 'No pain, no gain'. People push their bodies until they are hot, sweaty and exhausted, after which they need to eat and sleep in order to recharge their energy.

Qigong, as you will by now have realised, is *internal* training, connected with the Qi, the blood and the internal organs. When you practise Qigong you will not exhaust yourself, and – quite the opposite of what you experience in sports – the more you practise the more

Qi you will have and the more energetic you will become.

Of course, if you practise Qigong you will have more energy than you previously had to expend on the tennis court or football pitch. It is up to each individual to decide what they want out of their Qigong and sporting activities, and to find the right balance for themselves.

Qigong for children and adults

Another question I am often asked is: when is the best age to start practising? Again, this depends on each individual and the maturity of his or her mind. If you can understand the instruction, either from a teacher or from a book such as this, you can start – some children are ready at the age of seven or so, while other people need to wait until they are young adults.

8

Balancing Gong

Imitating animal movements

Balancing Gong is a Daoist Qigong exercise which mainly imitates the movements and daily life of animals. The exercises work by stimulating the Dantien to strengthen the back, shoulders and neck.

Nowadays, people have to sit for long periods in offices, cars, and so on. As a result in middle age their joints become stiff and painful, and sometimes even swollen. This is because of poor circulation. In Chinese medicine the Qi and the blood are connected. If the circulation is good then the Qi will be strong, the face will be a better colour, the skin soft and the joints more flexible. It all depends on your Qi.

In the body, all the organs are connected to the neck, spine and shoulders. The neck, spine and shoulders support the entire body and help to transfer the energy to the different organs. So if your neck has a problem, this will block the energy flow. Practising Balancing Gong can help your neck, shoulders and spine become stronger and more flexible.

Refer back to the diagrams on pages 24–25 for the positions of the acupuncture points.

Roc Extends Its Wings *(top) and* Monkey Walk *(right) are good examples of exercises based on animal movements.*

Holding the Dantien

THIS starting exercise stimulates the Dantien which stores the Qi. Placing your hands on your stomach connects the Laogong points at the centre of your palms to the Qihai point (about 1.5 cm below the navel) which relates to the Dantien.

1. ▼ Stand naturally, with your feet as wide as your shoulders. Keep your back straight and relax your shoulders and neck, keeping your head in an upright, natural position. (Unless stated otherwise, follow this starting position for all the exercises.)

2. ◀ Men should place their left hand on the Dantien, and the right hand over the left. Women should place their right hand on the Dantien with the left over it. Relax your whole body and lightly concentrate your thoughts on your Dantien.

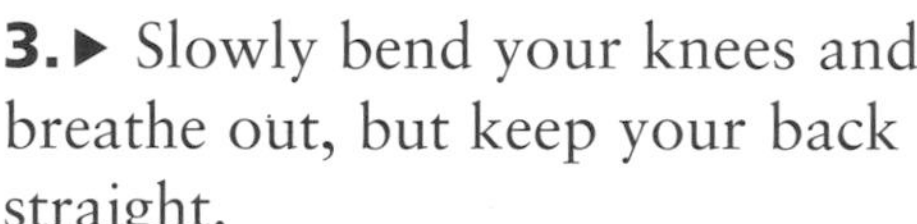

3. ▶ Slowly bend your knees and breathe out, but keep your back straight.

4. Slowly straighten your legs and breathe in.

The Dantien: up and down

THIS is good for your lungs, increases your breathing and stimulates your Dantien Qi by moving up and down.

1. Stand as in Step 2 of the previous exercise.

2. ▼ Separate your hands so the palms face upwards and the fingertips point towards each other. The hands should be level with the Dantien.

3. ◀ Slowly raise your hands from the Dantien to the chest, as high as the Qihu points on the upper chest, and breathe in.

4. ▼ Turn your palms down so the Hegu point on the hand faces the Qihu point (LEFT) and lower your hands back to the Dantien while breathing out and bending your knees (RIGHT).

Opening and closing the Dantien

THIS movement also stimulates the Dantien, and concentrates on breathing in and out with the Dantien.

1.▸ Stand naturally with your hands facing the Dantien (as if you were holding a small ball).

2. ◀ Turn your palms out (thumbs pointing down) and push your hands forwards and out. Meanwhile breathe in.

3. ▶ Turn your palms in and bring your hands back in towards the Dantien (as if you are squeezing the Qi into the Dantien); bend your legs and breathe out.

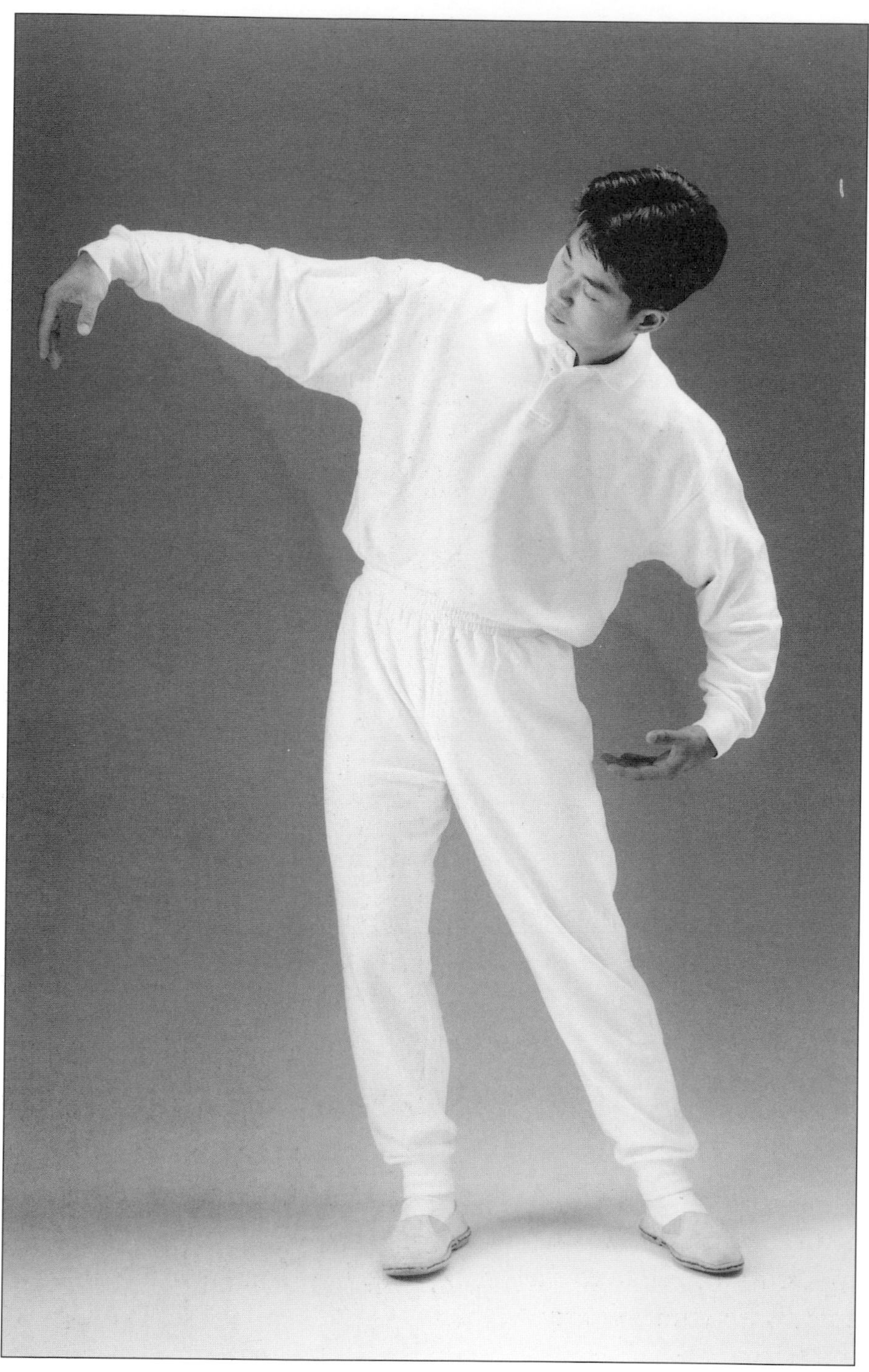

Turning the head and twisting the tail

THIS is good for the kidneys and helps you lose weight. Breathe in on either side, but breathe out on the opposite.

1. Stand naturally and relax your whole body.

2. ◀ Lean to the left while raising your right arm and bending your right leg. Keep your left leg straight but relaxed.

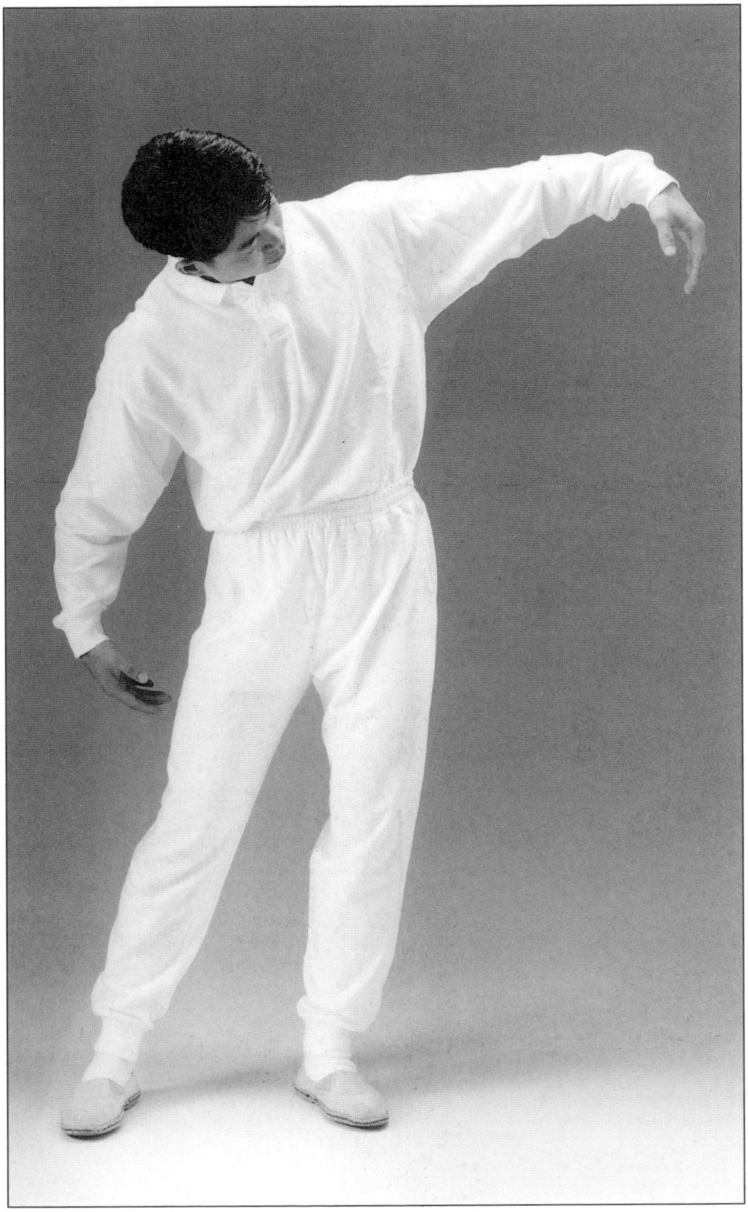

3. ▶ Do the same for the opposite side. Lean to the right, raise your left arm and bend your left leg.

Beautiful woman turns her waist

THIS exercise helps the back and kidneys, so if you are tired or have backache this is a good one to do. Afterwards your back should feel relaxed and warm. Remember to breathe naturally.

1. Stand naturally and relax your whole body.

2. ◂ Put your hands on your back, over your kidneys (as if you were holding them).

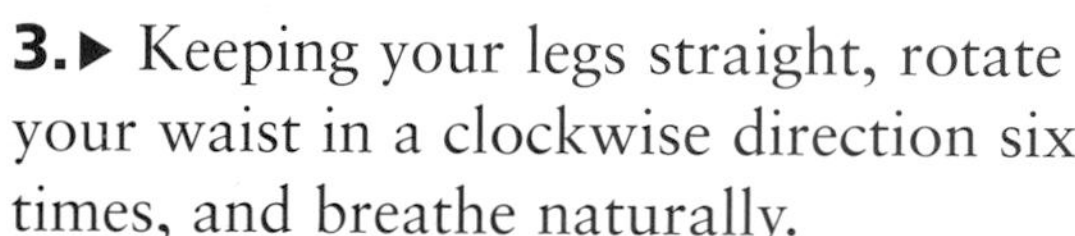

3. ▸ Keeping your legs straight, rotate your waist in a clockwise direction six times, and breathe naturally.

4. Rotate your waist six times in the other direction, i.e. anticlockwise.

Peeping monkey

THIS movement stimulates the Du Channel, which connects the whole spine. The Laogong point on the palm transmits the energy to the Yamen point on the neck. The exercise can cure backache and straighten the spine, making the body more upright. Breathing should be natural – breathe in on one side and breathe out on the other.

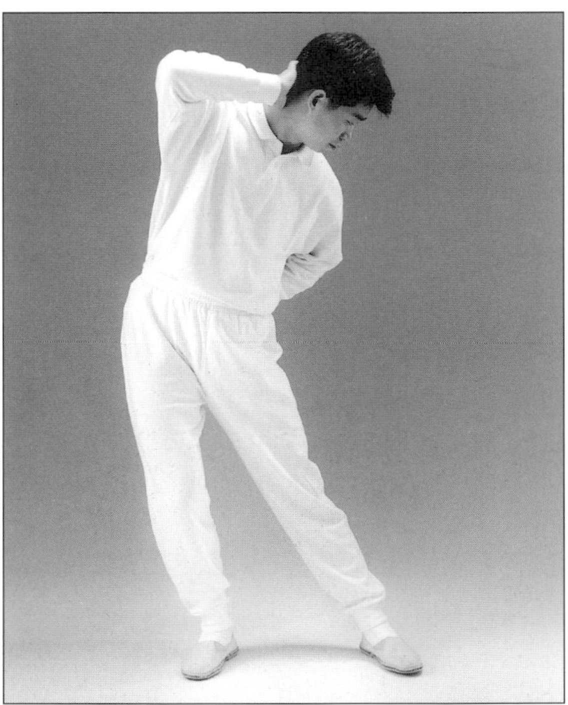

1. Stand naturally and relax your whole body.

2. ◀ Lean to the left, bend your right leg and relax your left leg.

3. ▶ Raise your right arm and with your fingers touch the Yamen point on the back of the neck. At the same time bring the left hand to the back, so the left Hegu point touches the Mingmen point on your back.

4. Repeat for the other side.

Big bear stretches

THIS movement 'rotates' your spine, shoulders and neck. When performing the exercise your internal organs move and so are exercised. The movement concentrates on the heart and stomach and strengthens your spine, shoulders and neck.

1. Stand naturally and relax your whole body.

2. ◂ Open your chest and lift up your shoulders. Breathe in.

3. ▸ Roll your shoulders forwards and down while closing your chest, bending your neck, back and knees. Breathe out.

4. Repeat Step 2.

Roc extends its wings

THIS movement is like a huge bird spreading its wings. It will help to strengthen your heart and lungs and to lift depression.

1. Stand naturally and relax your whole body.

2. ▼ Raise your arms out to the sides with the palms facing forwards.

3. ◀ Lean forwards and close your arms until the hands cross (either hand on top).

4. ▶ Lean back (not too far), bend your knees and open your arms and chest.

Supporting the sky

THIS is very good for the lungs and breathing as well as for backache. This movement is similar to stretching first thing in the morning.

1. Stand naturally and relax your whole body.

2.▸ Hold your hands in front of your Dantien so the palms face up and the fingers point to each other.

3.◂ Raise your hands up past the front of your chest so that the palms face the body and breathe in. As your hands come up, keep your back straight and when the hands reach the face roll your hands over (so the palms face upwards), and stretch your arms up.

4. ▼ Open your arms out to the sides and lower them down while bending the knees. Keep the back straight until the hands are in the starting position but now with your knees bent. Breathe out at the same time.

Cloud steps

THIS movement is a walking exercise. You should move as if you are walking on clouds and emphasise the movements. You can walk in any direction, and change direction any time you like. This one is good for arthritis and circulation because the walking soon makes you hot, which clears the 'poisons' from the joints. It is also good for your co-ordination.

1. Stand naturally and relax your whole body.

2. ◀ Lift your left arm and right leg, slightly bending your standing leg. Relax your right arm.

3. ▶ Lightly step forward with your right leg. Keep your left palm open, press down and breathe out.

4. ◀ Lift your right arm and left leg, and breathe in.

5. ▶ Continue walking slowly.

Monkey walk

THIS is another Walking Qigong exercise. By turning side to side, stimulating the Yamen point and Mingmen point (on the Du Channel) you strengthen your spine, shoulders and neck. You should walk in a circle, following the bagua, and so taking energy from all directions to cover the heart, lungs, kidneys and spleen.

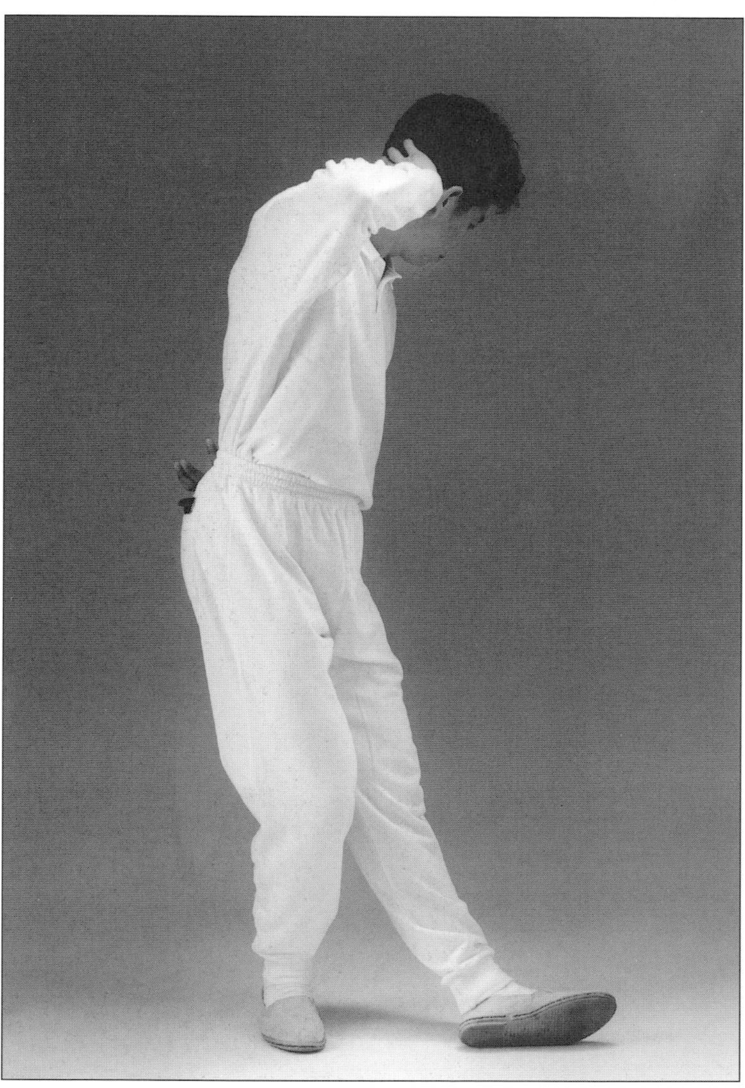

1. Stand naturally and relax your whole body.

2.◄ Lift your right hand and touch the Yamen point on the neck lightly with the fingers of the right hand. At the same time step forward with your left leg, placing the foot lightly on to the outside edge, so opening the Yongquan point on the sole. Your left hand should move to your back and the Hegu point touches the Mingmen point.

3. ◀ Close your left sole and shift your weight to your left leg, allowing it to bend at the knee. Relax both hands and drop them to your sides.

4. ▶ Repeat Step 2 for the opposite side.

9

Taiji Qigong

Many people will have heard of Taiji, which consists of beautiful movements and is good for the health. Actually Taiji originated in Northern China and belongs to the martial arts. Unfortunately it is not easy to learn – the sequences of the movements are complex and therefore difficult to pick up.

Taiji Qigong, however, consists of only eighteen movements taken from the Taiji forms, dance and daily life movements. They improve your health – in particular they strengthen your internal organs – and they allow you to treat your health problems yourself.

Taiji start

THIS movement is the same as the opening movement of many Taiji forms. When you perform it your whole body will be stimulated. The circulation becomes stronger, so the blood will flow through the joints and nourish them. This movement is therefore good for poor circulation and arthritis.

1. ▸ Stand naturally and relax your whole body.

2. ▾ Raise your arms to shoulder height and breathe in.

3. ▾▸ Slowly lower your hands until they are level with your waist. At the same time bend your knees and breathe out.

4. As in Step 2, raise your arms and at the same time straighten your legs and breathe in.

Opening the chest

WHEN you perform this movement it is as if you are opening the curtains to take in some fresh air. Keep your whole body relaxed. This movement will strengthen your heart and lungs and is good for reducing depression.

1. Stand naturally and relax your whole body.

2.▸ Raise your arms to shoulder height and breathe in.

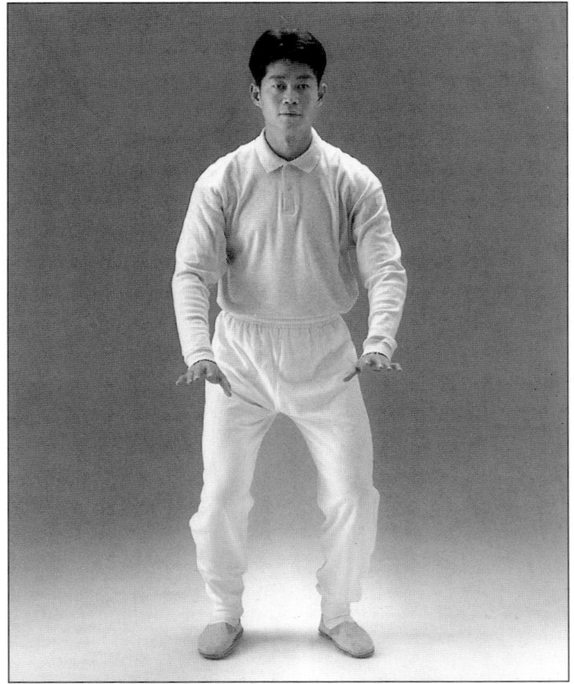

3. ▲◀ Keeping your joints relaxed, turn your hands so that your palms face your chest. Open your arms out to the sides, and breathe out.

4. ▲ Bring your arms back together so the hands are shoulder width apart with the palms facing one another, and breathe in.

5. ◀ Turn your palms to face downwards. Then slowly lower your hands until they are level with your waist. At the same time bend your knees and breathe out.

6. As in Step 2, raise your arms and at the same time straighten your legs and breathe in.

Rainbow dance

THIS movement looks like a lady holding two ribbons and waving her hands. It will make your stomach strong and help you to lose weight. It can also clear headaches because the Laogong point on the hand is transmitting the Qi to the Baihui point on the top of the head.

1. Stand naturally, with your feet slightly wider than your shoulders.

2. Lean to the left and bend your right leg.

3.▸ Raise your left arm to shoulder level and look at your left hand. Raise your right hand and hold it above your head so that the palm's Laogong point faces the top of your head and the Baihui point.

4. ▼ Lean to the right and bend your left leg. Let your right hand swing down to shoulder height and look at it. Bring your left hand up above your head.

5. Alternate between left and right, breathing naturally. Breathe in on either side and out on the other.

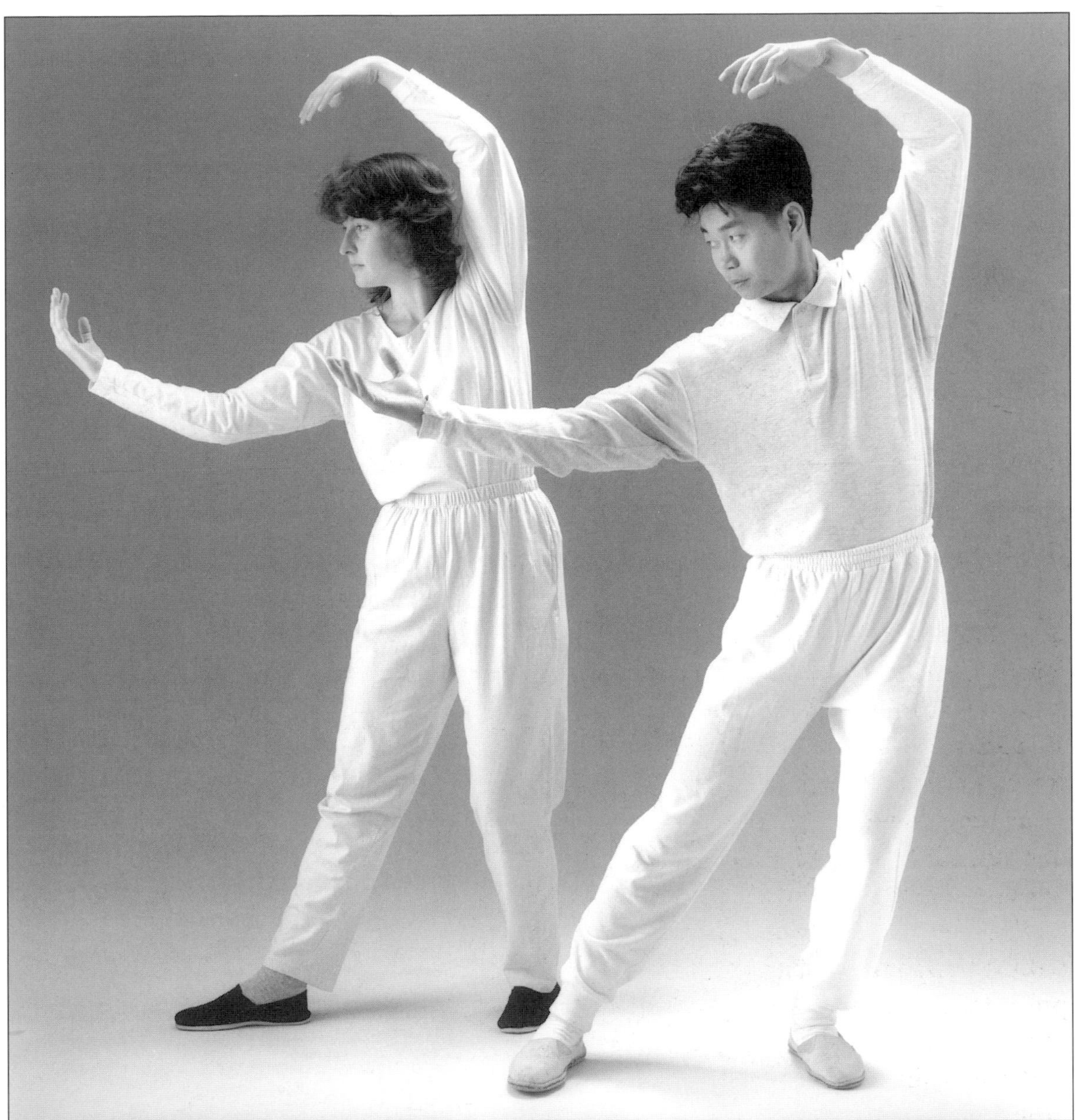

Rolling the arms

THIS is one of the full Taiji Quan movements. If you have done Taiji Quan before it will be easy, but if you are new to it you could move one hand first, then the other and finally both together. Once you get used to the movement you will like it because the sensation of Qi is very strong. Practising it will make your shoulders and neck flexible and you will lose weight. Because your hands are passing your chest it is also good for your lungs and heart. The more you move, the more you will relax – everything becomes very easy and harmonised. So, finally, it is good for reducing stress and panic. (This exercise is shown from the side for clarity).

1. Stand naturally and relax your whole body.

2.◄◄ (OPPOSITE PAGE) Keep your feet still and turn to the left. Raise your arms to shoulder height, right arm forwards and left arm pointing back, with both palms facing up. Look at your left hand.

3.◄ Bring your left hand up and towards you. Turn your body to face the front.

exercise continues

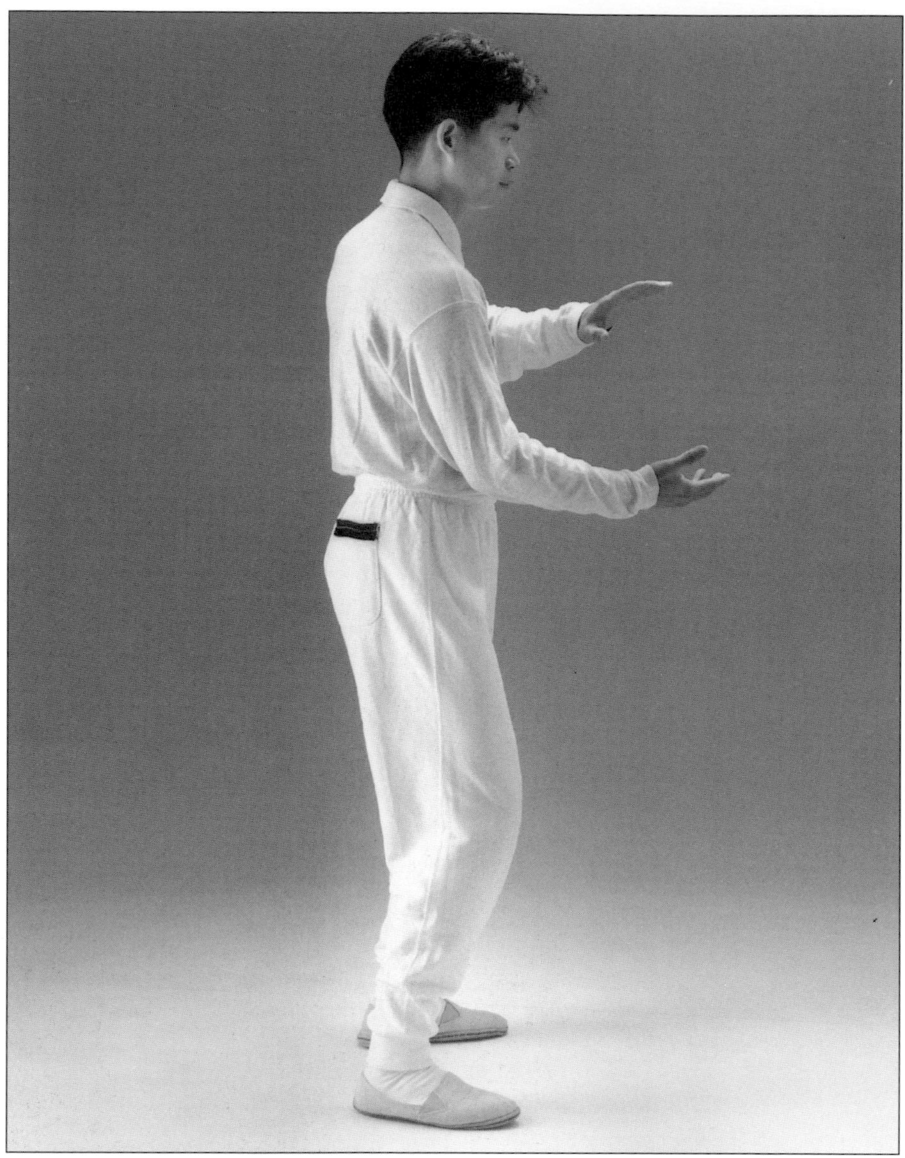

4. ▲ Bring both hands towards you so that the left hand, with the palm facing down, passes your head close to and just above your left ear, the Taiyang point, and your right hand drops slightly and comes to the centre (of your chest). After passing your ear your left hand should come to the centre, while your left palm should pass over the right just in front of your chest.

5. ◀ Turn to the right and push your left hand forwards.

6. ▼ Turn your right hand so that the palm faces down, and push your hand to the back. As your right arm begins to extend, turn both palms so that they face up.

7. Repeat for the right side.

Separating the clouds

THE Chong Channel and Ren Channel are at the centre and front of the body (see page 30). Practising this movement can help to stimulate these channels so that the Qi can run down to the Dantien, also opening the chest, strengthening the lungs and clearing blockages from the head.

1. Stand naturally and relax your whole body.

2. ▶ Slightly bend your knees. Hold your hands in front of the Dantien, one hand covering the other (men should hold their left hand nearest to their body, women should hold their right hand closest to the body). Keep your back straight.

3. ◀ Raise your hands in front of your body until your palms are above your head, and begin to straighten your legs. Meanwhile breathe in.

4. ▶ Turn your palms away from you. Separate your two hands so that they circle around and down and finish in front of the Dantien as in Step 2. As your hands circle down, bend your knees and breathe out.

Rowing the boat in the middle of the lake

IF YOU suffer from backache, tiredness or kidney problems this is a good exercise for you. But make sure you keep your legs straight and do not bend your head forwards lower than your waist – otherwise you will get dizzy.

1. Stand naturally and relax your whole body.

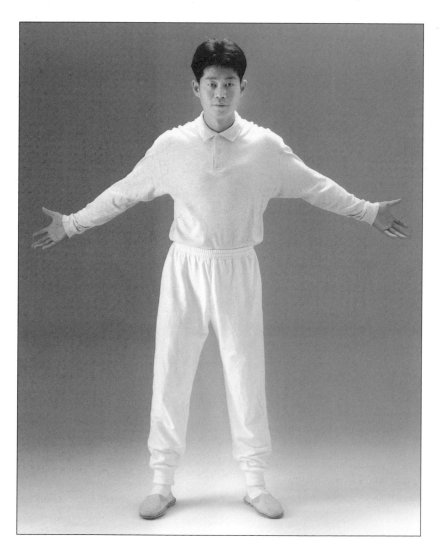

2.◂ Circle your arms slightly back and up, open your chest and breathe in.

3. ▶ When your arms are pointing up, bend forwards from the waist (keeping your back straight) and continue circling your arms forward and down. Breathe out.

4. When your arms point down, continue the circling motion, then straighten up and breathe in.

Lifting up the ball

THIS exercise should be performed with light, relaxed movements. It is as if you are gently bouncing a balloon with your hands to keep it in the air. Make sure your hands lift higher than your shoulders and that the back hand's Hegu point keeps facing the Huantiao point on the buttock to smooth the Gall Bladder Channel. This movement is good for the spirit, blood pressure and mind balance.

1. Stand naturally and relax your whole body.

2. Turn to the left and shift your weight to your left leg. Allow the right heel to lift off the floor.

3. ◀ Raise your right arm so that it crosses your body and the right hand is level with your left shoulder, palm facing up. Your left hand should move slightly left and back so that your left Hegu point faces the left Huantiao point. Look at your right hand.

4. ▲ Relax your body and turn your right palm over. Begin to swing your weight from your left leg to your right leg. At the same time drop your right hand down across your body to your back and bring your left hand up and in front of you.

5. ◀ You should end up in a position opposite to Step 3.

Turning the body to look at the moon

THE Chinese like the moon very much; that's why our calendar follows the lunar cycle. Many people like to come together as a family at night to enjoy the moonlight and listen to the older family members telling stories. In this movement you turn your body sideways by about 135 degrees, which strengthens the kidneys and stomach, improves the circulation and can help you to lose weight. Breathe in on either side, and out on the opposite side.

1. Stand naturally and relax your whole body.

2.▸ Turn to the left and shift your weight to your left leg. Allow your right heel to lift off the floor. Raise both arms to the left and side. Look in the same direction in which your hands are pointing.

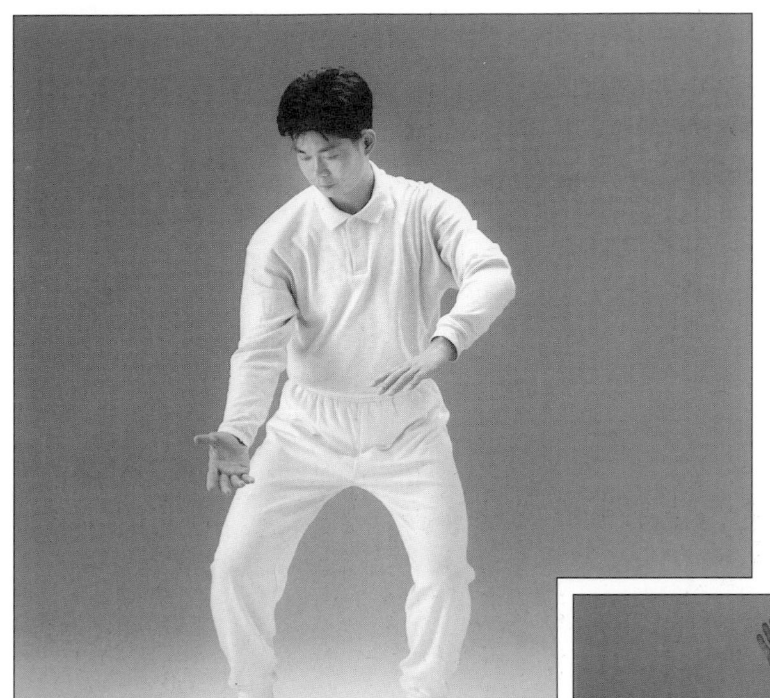

3. ◀ Relax your body and swing both arms down in front of you. Allow your knees to bend and begin to shift your weight from your left to your right leg.

4. ▶ Continue swinging your arms up to the right, finishing in a position opposite to that in Step 2.

Turning waist to pushing palm

THIS is a Taiji Quan movement, but we perform it differently since it is being used here for health purposes. Turning the waist strengthens your stomach and kidneys and opens the Dantien. Just make sure your palm comes from the centre when you push out. When you push with your left hand, it comes from the top of your crossed hands; but when you push with your right hand, this hand comes from on top. Again, breathe on alternate sides.

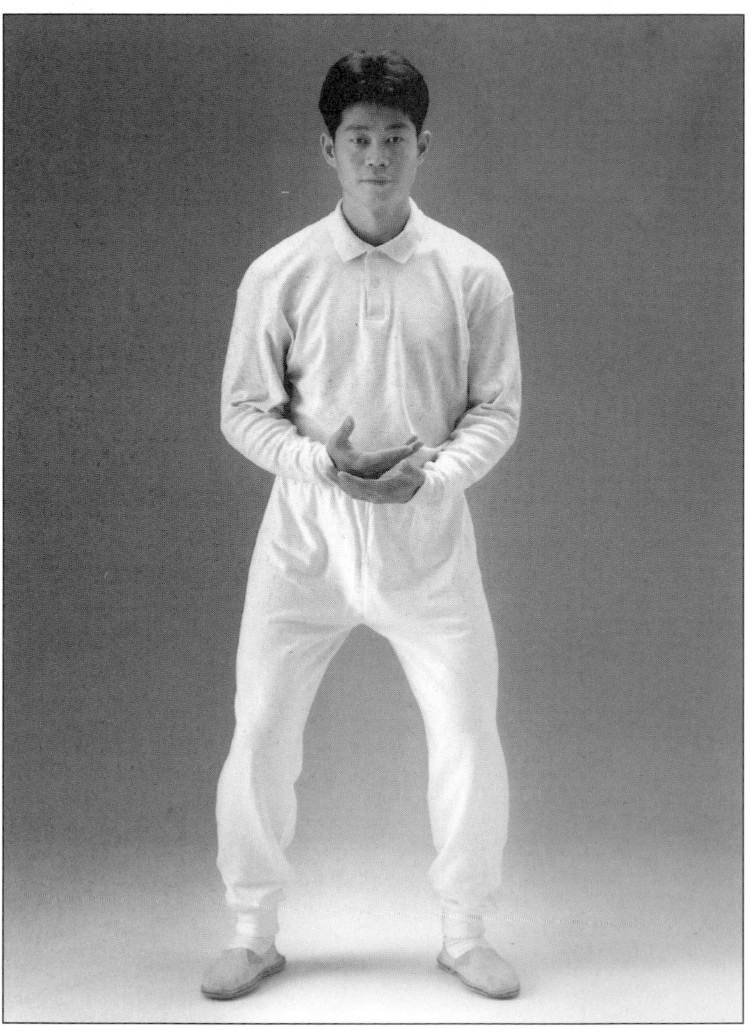

1. Stand with your feet slightly wider than your shoulders. Slightly bend your knees, but keep your back straight, as if you were riding a horse. Hold your hands loosely at your waist.

2.◂ Bring your hands up so that they cross in front of the Dantien (either hand can be on the inside).

3.▸ Turn to the left and bring your left hand back to your waist so that the Hegu point faces the Daimai point (on the Belt Channel) and then push your right hand out in front of you so that the right Hegu point faces your middle Dantien. Keep your legs relaxed and look at your right hand.

4. Withdraw the hands to their original position in front of the Dantien and turn to face the front.

5. Repeat for the right side.

Cloud hands in horse stance

CLOUD hands is a very common name in both Taiji and Qigong, and this too is a Taiji Quan movement. The hands follow the path of the same circle but in opposite directions.

Practising this movement will enhance your co-ordination, improve your mind balance and alleviate insomnia and arthritis. Move like a floating cloud, in a very relaxed way, and let the hands follow your waist. The hands should complete their circles at the same time. Move gently and slowly and look at whichever hand is on top. Breathe naturally – the more you can relax the more you will breathe with the movements.

At the beginning you might find it difficult to move both hands together so just move one hand first and then graduate to using both hands.

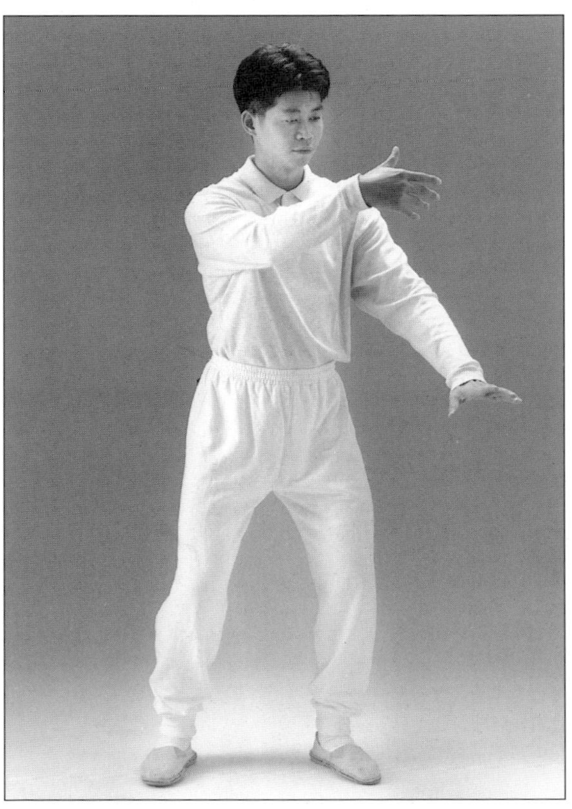

1. Again adopt a horse-riding position (see Step 1 of the previous exercise).

2.◂◂ (OPPOSITE PAGE) Hold your left hand in front of your left shoulder so that the elbow is slightly lower than your hand. The palm should face right and allow your waist to twist to the left slightly. Your right hand should start below the left hand, level with the Dantien, with the palm facing to the left.

3.◂ Turn the left palm to face the ground and press down to Dantien level. As the left hand drops, the right should rise.

exercise continues

4. ▼ Turn thc left palm to face the right and push in that direction. Allow the waist to twist slightly to the right. Stop when the hand is level with your right side. At the same time, your right hand moves across until it is in front of your right shoulder.

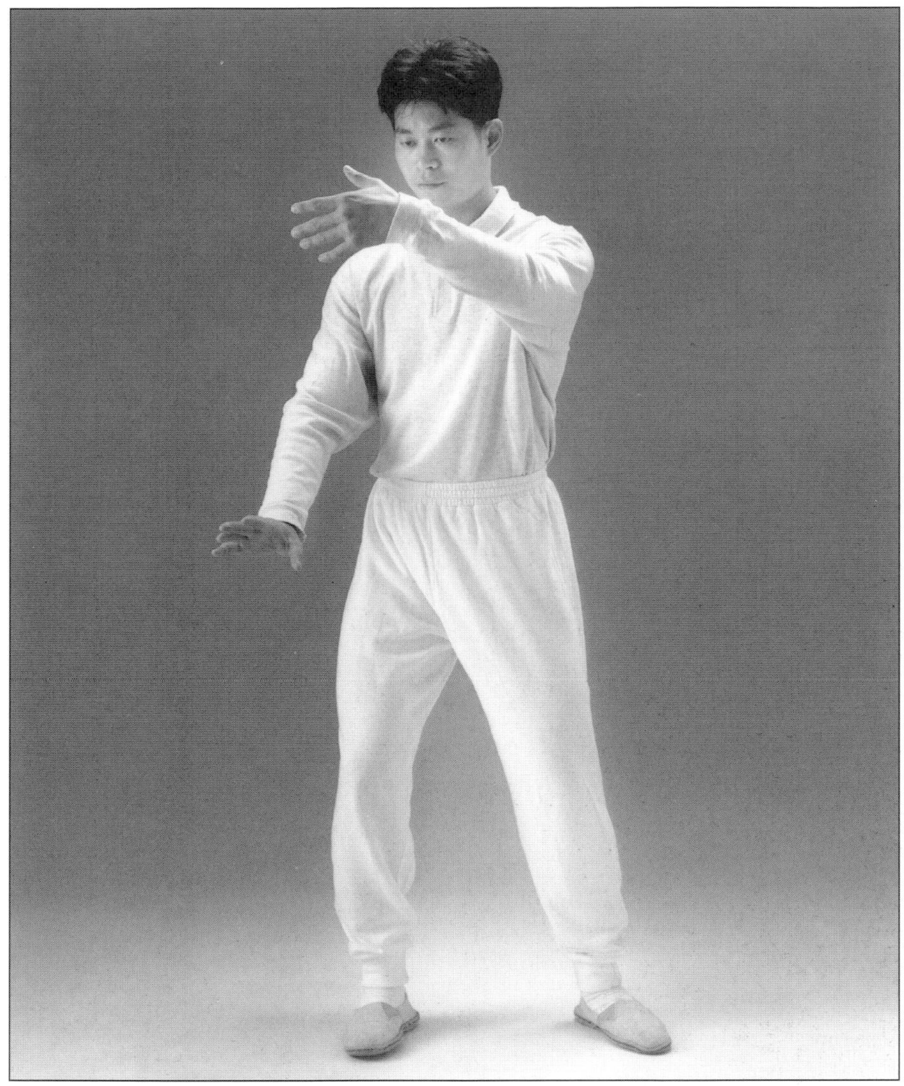

5. ▲ Relax your left wrist, letting the palm face downwards, and raise your hand, wrist first, to shoulder level. Your right hand moves down to Dantien level.

6. Let your left elbow drop slightly and turn your palm to face the right. With your wrist leading, slightly push to the left until your left hand is in its original position (see Step 2).The right hand moves across at the same time

Punching

THIS movement is like martial arts training, so some people do it quickly; but for health purposes we do it slowly in a relaxed manner. Then it strengthens our internal power and our legs – with strong legs our body will feel light. Breathe in on either side and out on the other.

1. ▼ Again adopt a horse-riding position and hold your fists, which should be loose, gently at your waist.

2. ◀ Punch gently forwards with one hand, letting your fist rotate as it moves forwards so that your thumb faces down. Stop before the arm is fully extended. Keep your back straight and your shoulders relaxed, and look forwards.

3. ▶ Withdraw your fist and repeat for the other hand.

Flying wild goose

IN THIS movement your arms are like the wings of a bird. Move gently and slowly and just look forwards, but do not focus on anything. The movement is very easy to do and strengthens the legs and kidneys.

1. Stand naturally and relax your whole body.

2. ◀ Raise your arms, elbows, wrists and then fingers to your sides, level with your shoulders, and breathe in.

3. ◀ Slowly drop your arms, elbows, wrists and then fingers, and bend your knees. Breathe out.

Rotating the wheel in a circle

THIS is like a big wheel in a funfair. It strengthens our back and makes it more supple. Make sure your legs are straight. Your breathing should be relaxed and natural. As your hands circle up you should breathe in, and as they come down you should breathe out.

1. Stand naturally and relax your whole body.

2. ▶ Bend forwards as far as possible.

3. ◀ Slowly swing your arms to the left, allowing your right hand to cross in front of your body. As your arms begin to circle left and up, allow your hands to turn so that your palms face outwards.

4. ▶ After your hands have passed over your head and are descending to your right begin to bend forwards from your waist. Keep your legs straight and don't move your feet. When your hands are pointing straight down you should be fully bent forwards.

5. Continue the motion and repeat the circle three times, then repeat the whole exercise for the opposite direction.

Pushing the wave

PUSHING waves is one of the full Taiji Quan movements, but it is slightly different here because we straighten the front leg when pushing the wave. In this movement the chest opens and is connected with the Qihu points in the stomach channel, so this exercise is good for the lungs and stomach. It is also beneficial for knee problems.

1. ▼ Stand with one leg forwards. Adopt a 'bow stance' so that your back foot turns out at 45 degrees while your front foot points forwards. Keep your weight on your back leg. Lift both arms to shoulder height.

2. ▼ Bring your hands in towards your chest so that your Hegu points face your Qihu points, palms facing down. Breathe in.

3. ▶ Sink down and move your weight forwards, with your palms pushing forwards at the same time. Shift your weight to your front leg and straighten it; your back leg goes up on its toes. Breathe out.

4. ◀ Relax your hands, palms facing downwards. Transfer your weight to your back leg and sink down. At the same time as you move your weight your hands return to the chest, Hegu points facing Qihu points. Breathe in.

5. Repeat six times, then change your front leg and repeat.

Flying pigeon

THIS movement is good for the lungs, the shoulders and the circulation. When you perform it, make sure the Laogong points come together when you close your arms. This will create a lot of heat in your palms and will cultivate your Qi.

1. Adopt a 'bow stance' (see *Pushing the wave*).

2. ◀ Open your arms out to your sides with your palms facing forwards. Transfer your weight on to your rear leg and allow the toes of your front foot to rise off the ground. Look forwards and breathe in.

3. ▶ Shift your weight forwards and close your arms in front of you. Shift your weight on to the front leg and allow the heel of the back foot to rise. Breathe out.

4. Repeat six times and then change the front leg.

Looking at the sky, touching the sea

THIS movement helps maintain the flexibility of the back and is good for circulation. It also opens the Baihui point on the top of the head which helps prevent headaches. (This exercise is shown from the side for clarity.)

1. Adopt a 'bow stance' (see *Pushing the wave*).

2. ▼ Open your arms out to your sides, with your palms facing forwards, and transfer your weight on to your rear leg. Keep the front foot flat on the floor and look forwards. Breathe in.

3. ▼▶ Shift your weight to your front leg and, while leaning forwards and downwards, close your arms and breathe out. Stop when you are fully forwards and your hands cross in front of your knee. Look at your hands.

4. Perform six times, then repeat for the other side.

Marching while bouncing the ball

拍

THIS movement is good for your brain as it tests your co-ordination and balance. Whenever we practise this movement it makes everybody laugh!

1. Stand naturally and relax.

2. ▼ In this movement your hands should gently move from your sides up in front of you, level with your shoulders. They should move in time with your legs, which should march on the spot. Each time lift your knees high enough to make your thigh horizontal. Begin by marching on the spot and lifting the same hand and foot e.g. the right hand and right foot.

3. ▼ Then at any time change the combination, e.g. right hand and left leg, or two steps on the right and one on the left, etc. The change should be smooth and relaxed.

Balancing Qi (Shou Gong)

AT THE end of every practice you should finish with Shou Gong to bring all the Qi back to the Dantien and store it there. It will also make you calm and relaxed.

1. Stand still with a slightly open stance.

2. ▼ Bring your hands to the Dantien, palms up and fingers facing each other.

3. ◀ Lift up your hands to your chest and rise up on your toes. Breathe in.

4. ▶ Turn your palms downwards, drop your heels and let your hands sink down to the Dantien. Breathe out.

10

Meditation

After finishing the movements of Qigong you need to do a quiet exercise – meditation. There are many different ways to meditate, both western and eastern, and meditation has a long history, related in particular to religion. These forms of meditation emphasise the 'heart and the spirit'.

What are the benefits?

The main reasons why people meditate today are to relax and recharge their energy, but there are actually more benefits than this to be gained. If you achieve a high level of meditation, the Chinese believe you can heal all your illnesses. One example is a friend of my teacher Yip Chun (who taught me the martial art of Wing Chun).

This friend had been suffering from a chronic disease for many years. People would turn away when he spoke to them because of the bad smell coming from his body. Doctors said that his lungs were very seriously damaged and that he would not live very long.

Thirty years after the illness had first been discovered, my teacher went back to his home town of Foshan in China, and saw his old friend again. But this time the friend looked very healthy, with a rosy face, and he had survived to reach the age of seventy. He said, 'I knew my health was not good, so I practised some Buddhist style meditation which I learned at school. At first I did half an hour a day, then slowly increased it to an hour, and now I wake up every morning at five o'clock and do my meditation until nine o'clock. Four hours every day, and now I have recovered.' In his meditation he uses a Full Lotus (see below), with his palms and the soles of his feet facing up to the sky. This helps all the negative energy to come out through his palms and soles and recharges his positive energy.

By doing meditation we also develop our healing powers, because it helps us transmit Qi to weak and sick people. During meditation you will feel the Qi flowing inside your body. When all the channels are clear the Qi will be very strong. Outside, the body feels soft, all the muscles and joints are relaxed; and this means the inside is strong (when the outside is Yin, the inside must be Yang). You cannot only feel the Qi but you will also see it. There are many different colours that come from our internal organs. You can see many different things – more than just with the eyes.

The mind is more powerful than the eyes and the body. Wherever you want to go is limited, but your mind can go even beyond the universe – wherever you imagine you can go. At the highest level of meditation you bring yourself to be nothing – called Wu Wai. Then you become one with the universe, you go back to your own natural orbit and to your own rhythm. At that stage illness, damage and any other problems will be cleared by your Qi.

Full Lotus Posture

Many people practise their own style of meditation, sitting, standing, lying or in the lotus position. Some even use gestures or mantras. However, they still remain conscious of themselves – they cannot let go of their mantras to forget everything. It is like drinking tea – you have finished, but you are still holding your cup.

Here are ten different methods of concentrating to prepare for meditation.

Concentration

1. IMAGINATION
Imagine the moon at the centre of your body, in your Dantien. Clouds drift slowly past and the moon disappears behind them, then it appears again. Combine this visualisation with your breathing.

2. REFLECTION
Imagine an object you like, such as a flower, a tree, the sun, the moon or a person, and put this visualisation in your Dantien.

3. WATCHING
Look at one object and forget everything else.

4. LISTENING
Imagine a sound like a steam train slowly pulling away in the distance, water dropping or a clock ticking.

5. MUSIC
You can listen to some beautiful music during meditation to bring yourself to a relaxed state.

6. COUNTING THE BREATH
Breathe in and breathe out while counting the length of each breath.

7. READING
Think of a poem or phrase (similar to mantra repetition).

8. CONCENTRATION
Let the distractions come and slowly achieve balance through concentrating on them.

9. LOCATION
Go to a peaceful place, let the atmosphere influence you, and then practise meditation.

10. NUMBERS
Count from one to a hundred during meditation.

All these methods will help you to achieve a quiet state and forget everything. In the beginning everyone has a problem with concentrating the mind, so: 'Use one thought to get rid of a thousand thoughts until everything is peaceful.'

STANDING POSITIONS *(Zhan Zhong)*

1. Three small circles standing position

STAND still, with your legs as wide as your shoulders. Bend your knees and raise your hands as if you were holding a ball in front of your Dantien. Your palms should face your Dantien so that your Laogong points face your Dantien. Close your eyes and choose one of the concentration methods. Then relax.

Bring your mind to your Dantien, then at the end forget everything. If you find that your body moves, control it. This is not Spontaneous Qigong, so the body should not move. If your arms or joints feel stiff you can adjust your position a little.

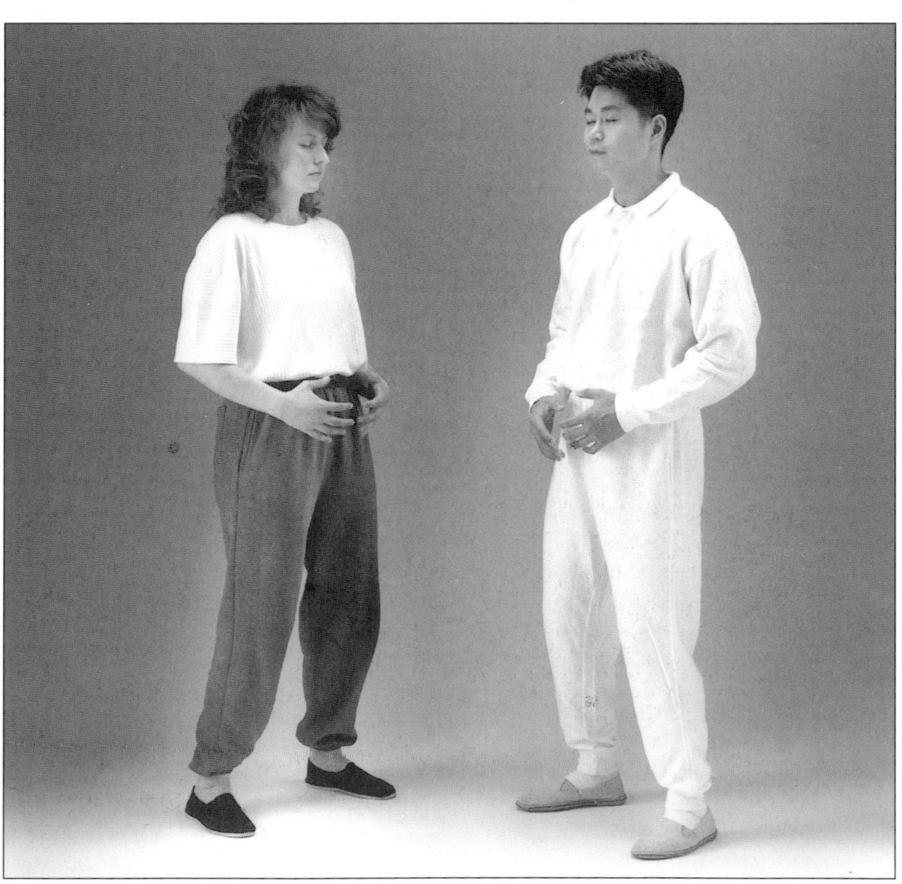

2. Pressing down standing position

AS ABOVE, but only lift your hands to either side of your waist with the palms (Laogong points) facing the ground. This will release the negative Qi to the earth. The positive Qi will come up from your Dantien to your Baihui point. This is good for a tired or weak body.

SITTING POSITIONS

3. Holding a circle sitting on a chair

SIT forwards on the edge of a chair letting the air pass across your back. Bend your knees and keep your feet flat on the ground. Keep the knees and toes vertically in line as this helps the circulation in the legs. With your back straight, relax your shoulders, close your eyes and your mouth (keep the tip of your tongue touching between the upper palate and the root of the teeth – if you close your mouth, everything should be in the correct position). Hold your hands in front of the Dantien, left hand on top for men and right hand on top for women (this is because the Qi

flows differently for men and women), with the thumbs touching as if you were holding a small ball. Totally relax your body and choose one of the concentration methods. Then bring your mind to your Dantien and finally forget everything. (This exercise can also be done sitting in the lotus position.)

4. Holding Qi with purely Yang

SIT AS before. Raise your hands, palms facing, so that the upper and lower arms are at right angles and the armpits are open. Then relax your whole body, close your eyes and mouth, and concentrate on your Dantien.

LYING MEDITATION

1. Holding the Dan by lying flat

LIE ON your back with a pillow under your head so you can sleep comfortably and can keep the Qi flowing smoothly through your body. Close your eyes and mouth and open your legs slightly. Place your left hand on your Dantien and your right hand over it (opposite way fround for women) and then concentrate on your Dantien.

2. Bow sleeping

LIE ON your side (left side to improve the liver and heart and right side for the kidneys and lungs). Put the bottom hand under your head and the other hand on your legs. Slightly bend the bottom leg, which allows the Qi to flow strongly. (See photograph below.)

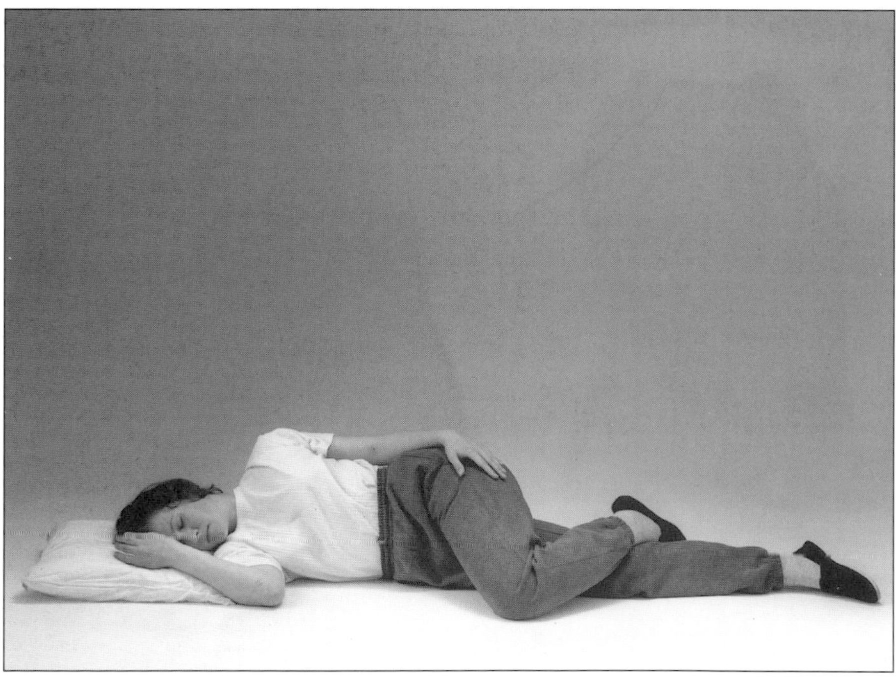

From the Tang to the Song Dynasty (AD 618 – 1127) lived Chen Bo, a very famous Daoist. His sleeping method enabled him to go for months without waking up. Once a woodcutter passed through Hwa Shah, where Chen Bo lived, and there saw what he thought was a dead body lying on the ground. But when he touched it he found it was very warm and the heart was still beating. After a while Chen Bo said, 'Why did you disturb me? I was sleeping very well!' The Tang Emperor Shi Zong (AD 956) invited Chen Bo to come to the palace. Immediately on arrival, Chen Bo went to his room, closed his door and fell asleep. A month later he woke up, and only then did he see the Emperor! Sleeping made him healthy and enabled him to develop his Daoist method.

For any meditation, first get the correct posture and then relax the body. When you don't feel relaxed you have a blockage or injury, so you must try to relax that area more. No matter how you feel, let everything happen and just keep relaxed. Maybe you will feel warm, tingling or itchy – such sensations are very natural. Also you will find that saliva forms in your mouth. Swallow it, because it can help to balance your internal body.

When you meditate don't think of the time, but just go on for as long as you feel comfortable. When you want to finish your meditation, you should complete with Shou Gong, which means Ending Exercise or Collecting or Balancing Exercise. No matter what kind of Qigong you practise, you must always do this as it brings your Qi back to the Dantien to store it so it is not lost. If you have been meditating in a sitting or lying position you should do the Shou Gong sitting (see following photographs). If you have been meditating standing up, you should do the Shou Gong standing too.

Shou Gong

1. ▸ Start to open your eyes. Rub your hands together until they feel warm.

2. ◂ Then 'wash' your face three times with your hands passing over your eyes, your nose, the top of your head and your ears.

3. ▶ Open your arms out to your sides.

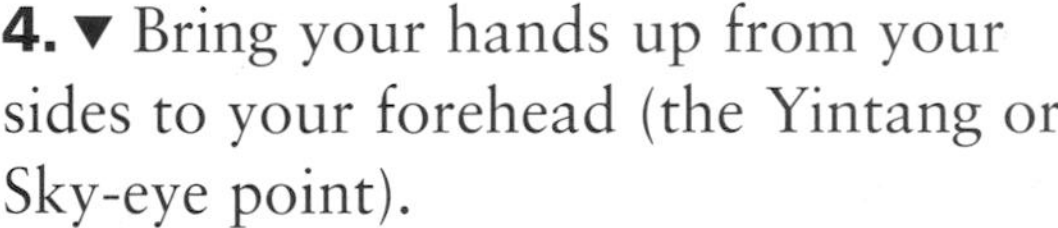

4. ▼ Bring your hands up from your sides to your forehead (the Yintang or Sky-eye point).

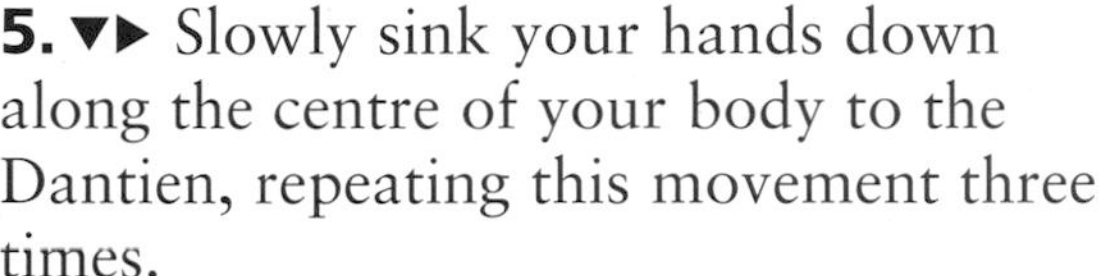

5. ▼▶ Slowly sink your hands down along the centre of your body to the Dantien, repeating this movement three times.

A Final Word

I have been practising Qigong and martial arts for around twenty years but still, after all this time, I find I have a long way to go. Chinese skills are like a big tree. You pull a leaf, and think you have a good hold of it, but then you find it is connected to a twig, which is connected to a branch, which is in turn connected to the trunk, then the trunk is connected to the roots which spread out and even connect to other trees. It never stops. Personally, I find it is not how much knowledge you have that is important, but how your knowledge helps and improves your life.

When studying something, I always say this is only one of the ways you can go. You will understand this particularly if you understand Chinese philosophy which tells us there are many ways which lead to the same destination. I remember an occasion when I was working in Hong Kong and my boss told me I was wrong. I replied, 'There is no right and no wrong.' He just looked at me and didn't say a word but, of course, when he wrote my report he didn't treat me very favourably! However, finding there are many different ways does not mean we can do anything we like. There is actually a certain principle underneath that never changes. If it does, the destination changes, or there might be side effects that could cause problems for you. This principle is 'nature'. Whichever way you choose, the principle should never change – it is the centre, the key. This is also the best way to study Qigong. No matter what kind of Qigong it is, it is important to follow nature, to be natural. One reason some people think Qigong is secret and dangerous is because they try to reach a high level as quickly as possible and this causes problems.

There is an old story in China about a farmer. The farmer was very jealous of his neighbour whose rice always grew faster and taller than his. So one night he crept out into his own field and pulled at the rice. He thought by pulling it he would make it grow quicker. When he had finished, he went home to bed feeling very pleased with himself. The next day he got up and went out to see his rice, expecting to see it standing tall and strong. But, when he got there he was very upset – it had all died. How stupid he had been! This story tells us success needs time and effort, not just luck. If luck comes and you stop working, everything will be lost. Practising Qigong is the same – it takes time and effort.

Finally, one good reason for practising Qigong which I'd like to mention is to do with the environment. Air is an element of Qi and by practising we are helping to do something good for nature, for the world around us. I've already spoken about the importance of doing Qigong in fresh air, but as well as taking from the air, we can help put something back. By letting strong, healthy Qi circulate we can help enrich the quality of the increasingly polluted air around us. Let's do something positive for future generations!

Tse Qigong Centre

The Tse Qigong Centre offers genuine, high quality information to all those who wish to develop their Qigong. The Centre started in 1991 and over two thousand people have benefited from it. Over the three years it has been running, the centre has gained in popularity and has attracted many people, including western doctors, acupuncturists, homeopaths, herbalists, teachers of Taiji Quan and martial arts, etc.

The Tse Qigong Centre holds regular classes, seminars, lectures and treatments that are given either by myself, or my instructors. Classes are offered in:

Dayan Qigong: A very beautiful Qigong exercise that stimulates the acupuncture points and channels, using the Qi to heal yourself and eliminate negative Qi.

Chen Taiji Quan: The original form of Taiji Quan that has both gentle and slow movements together with strong and fast movements using spiralling energy. With the form, 'pushing hands' and weapons are taught to develop both health and martial art.

Wing Chun Kuen: This is a high level martial art technique developed by a woman – Yim Wing Chun. The art has a very profound philosophy behind it, and uses less strength to overcome a stronger opponent.

The Centre also publishes *Qi Magazine* which offers up-to-date information and high quality articles on Qigong, martial arts, *Yi Jing* (*I Ching*), Feng Shui, Chinese horoscopes and philosophy. The magazine has topics for both the beginner and those looking for more detailed information about Chinese culture and skills.

Further Information

For a full list of approved and certified Tse Qigong Centre instructors, please visit our website at:

www.qimagazine.com

or call
UK: 0161 929 4485

Tse Qigong Centre
PO Box 59
Altrincham WA15 8FS
Tel 0161 929 4485
Fax 0161 929 4489
tse@qimagazine.com

Index

Exercise headings appear in **bold type.**